NEVER
UNFRIENDED

NEVER
UNFRIENDED

The Secret to **Finding** and **Keeping** Lasting Friendships

(in)courage community manager
LISA-JO BAKER

B&H
PUBLISHING GROUP

NASHVILLE, TENNESSEE

978-1-4336-4306-4

Published by B&H Publishing Group
Nashville, Tennessee

Dewey Decimal Classification: 177
Subject Heading: FRIENDSHIP \ HUMAN BEHAVIOR \
FEMALE FRIENDSHIP

1 2 3 4 5 6 7 8 • 21 20 19 18 17

For every woman I've been honored to call *friend*.
Thank you for that gift.

CONTENTS

HOW WE DEFINE FRIENDSHIP IN THIS BOOK—IT MIGHT NOT BE WHAT YOU THINK

I HAVE SPENT THOUSANDS OF hours of my life held hostage by worry about friendships. I have overanalyzed, ranted, and kept my husband awake as I rehashed interactions with women I care about—mining our conversations for minute details and trying to make sense of who was wrong and whether or not I needed to apologize or if I was justified in feeling so upset.

I have worried just as much about misunderstandings with women I didn't even know on a first-name basis.

I have cried in hidden corners of hotel lobbies over throwaway sentences that still managed to cut deep, and panic-checked my phone in the middle of the night for text messages. I have woken up first thing in the morning to squint at my emails in order to determine if an argument has escalated or finally been resolved. And I've walked through long days under the weight of dread that comes with unresolved conflict. I have hit refresh hundreds of times on Facebook to see who has included me, criticized me, or misunderstood me.

No matter what else has been going on around me, I've paused my life, my kids, my focus in church, my pot of boiling pasta, my work, my errands, my car, and at times even my anniversary celebrations in order to obsessively track what other people are saying about me. And I have wished I could control what they're thinking about me too.

I have been afraid and resentful. I have wanted to hide. I have felt sorry for myself. I have been so full of jealousy I could almost feel it—like black, thick, greasy tar clogging up my soul. And I have wanted to blame the women around me for how terrible I've felt on my secret insides.

Friendship is not for the faint of heart.

Because nothing hurts as much as the unkind words of a friend.

And I know I'm not the only one who feels this way.

I've heard too many stories, cried with too many women, and apologized too many times to think I'm the only one with these bruises on my heart and holes in my story where friends fell through.

I'm guessing you can relate?

I'm guessing that, like me, while on the outside you might look like a grown-up—maybe even with kids of your own—there's a teenage girl who lives inside you just like the one who lives inside me. Mine has long, stringy hair and ears that embarrass her because once upon a time a hairdresser told her they stick out too far from her head.

The teenager inside our grown-up bodies still worries about fitting in, being included and what her friends think of her. She worries what people will think of her ears or maybe the tiny apartment she grew up in, her old acne scars or her struggle to make sense of math. Not to mention her fashion sense and whether or not she's comfortable in the body she's grown up into. And while she might look put together on the outside, she's wondering if the "cool kids" notice her. Because she notices them noticing everyone else and she's not sure how to make herself worthy of being included, invited, and loved.

I don't know about you, but the last time I dressed up to seriously impress a man was when my husband and I were still in the do-you-notice-me-not-noticing-you-noticing-me phase.

But the last time I dressed up to impress another woman was yesterday morning when I painstakingly blow-dried my hair before escorting a group of kids on a field trip to the farm.

To. The. Farm.

My son's teacher is the opposite of me in every way. She is petite and effort-lessly fashionable with truly great hair. So 7:30 a.m. found me determined to tame my own unruly mane. There may also have been eyeliner and a cute purse involved.

No one can make us quite as unsure about ourselves as another woman.

We can stand knee-deep in witty conversation holding cupcakes in one hand and our highly connected smart phones in the other—only to go home and whisper in quiet tears to our husbands, our roommates, or our moms how left out we felt.

We want to matter to the people we think matter. We want the people we think matter to single us out. We want them to want to spend time with us. We want them to want to share bits of themselves with us that they don't share with anyone else. We want them to invite us in.

Into the shared secrets and secret Facebook groups. Into the late-night conversations and preschool play dates. Into the weekend getaways or playground pick-up routines. Into the Bible studies and co-ops. Into the conferences and moms' groups, into the planning committees, study groups, and vacation plans.

We want in.

Left on the wrong side of the door, we can regress into eighth grade versions of ourselves in mere minutes. We worry that we're too tall, too short, too uncool or unfashionable or uncomfortable in our own skins to fit in. Or that we're too loud or too quiet or too much or too little.

There is a voice that whispers all the reasons we deserve to be out—a voice that taunts. There is a voice that relentlessly lists every time we've found ourselves on the outside and actually revels in each remembering.

There is a mean girl inside us all who will hypnotize us if we let her. She will poison and paralyze our friendships by focusing on the moments when we felt excluded. She will trick us into thinking that there's an inner circle we've been left out of. She will repeat the lie that we've been left out on purpose. And maybe, painfully, sometimes we have.

Everyone is on the outside of something, but that is only half the story. The good news is that we are all on the inside of something—often without even realizing it.

That's what this book is about.

It's about looking deep into the eyes of that teenager inside you, cupping your hands gently around her tender, confused face, and pointing her in the direction of all the IN that's waiting for her. All the ways she's wanted. All the ways she belongs. If she's willing. If she's willing to stop keeping score and making lists of who's in and who's out, and if she will begin to do the terrifying work of letting people see her naked insides. And scarier yet, if she's willing to make the first move or, even worse, the hundredth move of starting over and over and over and over again at being the friend she wants.

Because no matter how invisible you feel or how well you are known, I have yet to meet another woman who doesn't have scars from broken friendships. In a world where we can be unfriended with the swipe of a finger, sometimes as recently as yesterday, those scars can defeat us. They can isolate us. And we can become experts at cutting people out of our lives just so we don't have to deal with the discomfort of being their friend.

However, the ultimate friend, Jesus—the One who moved into the neighborhood to get to know us, the friend of the popular and unpopular, of priests and pastors, of the uneducated and the graduated, of elementary school girls and their minivan-driving moms—put it pretty plain and simple. When asked what the greatest commandment was, He said,

"Love the Lord your God with all your heart, with all your soul, and with all your mind. This is the greatest and most important command. *The second is like it: Love your neighbor as yourself. All* the Law and the Prophets depend on these two commands" (Matt. 22:37–40, emphasis mine). The book of Luke picks up this thread in a conversation between Jesus and a legal scholar who also quoted this commandment.

But when the scholar pressed Jesus to define *who exactly* this neighbor is that we're commanded to love, Jesus didn't give an inch. He gave a story. And it defines neighbor not as a particular *who*, but instead as a *what*, as in *what you should do*. The parable of the good Samaritan isn't about identifying your neighbor; it's about *being* a neighbor. In essence, it's about being the kind of friend you wish you had.

In Luke 10, Jesus tells the story of a man who gets mugged and left for dead on the side of the road. (Or maybe in our case, the woman who gets beat up by the verbal attacks of the Internet, her roommates, the other mothers on the PTA, or her church family.) And instead of offering help, Jesus describes two people who literally looked the other way and kept right on walking. Two people who, according to their job descriptions, should have been the first to stop and care and comfort.

Instead, it's the one person Jesus' audience never would have expected who stops and loads up the stranger, takes him to the nearest hotel, and pays for his room, food, and care. The Samaritan is the unlikeliest helper in this scenario because he's the one that Jesus' audience—the Jewish religious elite, the famous, feted, and privileged—had ridiculed, rejected, and cut out of any invitations to participate in worship at their most sacred sites.

The Samaritan is the one person who would have been justified in holding on to his bitterness and rejection and ignoring the person in need of a friend.

But instead, the Samaritan in Jesus' story physically embodied the second greatest commandment. Without judgment, without squeamishness, and with wholehearted generosity, the Samaritan loved this stranger/neighbor as himself. And myself doesn't want to be left alone when I'm hurting. Myself doesn't want to be rejected, uninvited, or abandoned. Myself desperately wants to be seen and feel connected and have people ache with me when I ache and celebrate with me when I celebrate.

That's the heart of this book—the call back to friendship—even when it's hard, awkward, unfamiliar, or scary. Being willing to be a neighbor in the heart sense of the word is being willing to connect with the people who God puts in our path. It's doing life together, especially the hard parts. It's choosing friendship on purpose.

Being a friend, like being a neighbor, requires action on our part. So instead of asking, "Who is my friend?" this book will be asking, "How can I *be* a friend?" That's a radical shift in how our culture defines friendship. But I'm convinced that by the end of our time together, it will actually be a relief to have permission to spend less energy obsessing about "me" and my world of worries and records of wrongs done to me. And more time to spend interested in "her"—the friend I want to love as myself. Because the more I focus on her, the less space is left in my head to obsess over my own hurts, faults, and rejections. It's a relief to stop thinking about myself and start loving someone else.

This book isn't the magic formula to fixing all your friendships. There will be some things that we can't change about our friendships and some things that we can. But it is an invitation for you to model friendship on the one friend who has promised to never unfriend us. So we'll share real time, practical secrets to finding and keeping lasting friendships. And it might be much simpler and also more difficult than you think. Because whether we take the first step toward someone else is entirely up to us. While we might have defined friendship our whole lives by what others do to us, in the end it's what we do for others that will define us as friends or not. That's how we get friendship to stick. And that's what this book is about.

> *While we might have defined friendship our whole lives by what others do to us, in the end it's what we do for others that will define us as friends or not.*

I am in my forties, and I'm slowly learning this life lesson. I'm so glad we get to learn it together. Whether you're twenty-one or sixty-two, whether you're a minivan-driving mom, a college student, a work-from-home entrepreneur, a junior high girl facing finals, or a grandma with a gaggle of grandkids. Whether you've never had a close friend or you're currently tight with a BFF, this book is for all of us. Because we need each other. We women need each other. So let's do this. Let's reclaim our heritage of friendship we can trust with women we can depend on. Especially on our bad hair days and sleepless nights. Let's go be the friends that last.

How to Use This Book—Start Anywhere!

This book is your friend. It wants to make life easier and friendship less scary. This book does not want to be the boss of you. It wants to be your companion. Your cheerleader. Your encourager and your Sherpa on the journey back into friendship. And because I know that each awesome woman holding this book in her hands is at a different stage of that journey, I want to encourage you to jump right into the chapters that most meet you where you are right now.

So if your today looks full of fear, hurt, and uncertainty. Or if your nights are spent stressing instead of sleeping because a friend didn't text you back or because of an invitation you didn't get. Or if you're obsessing about what you said or didn't say or what you think she thinks you said, go right ahead and flip to *Part 1: What Are We Afraid Of?* In this section, we unpack the family of all our worst friendship fears. Those fears that seem to travel as a pack anytime we're trying to connect with other women. You're not the only one who struggles with these fears. Truly. Come learn about them and find out how to recover from things like friendship PTSD, the paralyzing fear of being left out, or the cringe-inducing awkwardness of always being the new girl or the girl who doesn't fit in.

Maybe you find yourself in a continual paranoid guilt cycle about that friend you always seem to disappoint, or you're feeling disappointed again by that one person you thought you could count on. If this is your reality at the moment, then maybe you should start in *Part 2: What* Can't *We Do about It?* Because the truth is, when it comes to friendships, there are some things we just can't fix. Period. Some things that aren't even our job to try and fix. So if you need off the hamster wheel of trying to make a friendship work that just will not cooperate, we'll meet you in Part 2.

Let's reclaim our heritage of friendship we can trust with women we can depend on.

What if you're looking for practical advice on how to actually initiate friendships, connect with other women, and be seen, known, and valued? *Part 3: What* Can *We Do about It?* is where you want to start. This is where you'll receive real-life advice for actually doing what seems to come naturally to kids on the playground—making genuine friends. This section is full of life-giving, countercultural suggestions for what we can do to get out of our own way, build a bridge into someone else's life, and actually follow through on that wild hope for friends who get us, love us, and stick by us.

Part 4: Where Do We Start? takes initiating friendships a step further by prodding you to get started. Because friendship, like all hard and worthwhile things, takes practice. Part 4 is where we start practicing together.

Right from the start you have permission to break the rules. To jump in and out of chapters. To underline and mark up the pages and rip out the ones that speak loudest to you and tape them up on your bathroom mirror. For real. We get that friendship can start to make you feel crazy and we hope that by the end of this book you'll feel such a great sigh of relief knowing you're not alone when it comes to figuring all this stuff out. Not alone by a long shot.

PART 1

WHAT ARE WE AFRAID OF?

"I'm so afraid of not fitting in that I avoid even trying. I'm so used to living this way that it's hard to change." —Beth[1]

The thing about fear is how claustrophobic it is. On days when I feel fear pressing in, everything about my life shrinks. While joy makes me want to throw my arms out wide, throw back my head, and grin into the sunshine like a giant oak tree that is waving with abandon at the wind, fear makes me cringe. Fear makes me want to hide. Fear makes me afraid of my own gifts and name. Instead of sharing them with the world, fear makes me want to dig a hole and stuff all that I am and all that I love deep down into the dark where no one can get to them.

Fear is a terrible friend.

Fear is wretched at friendship.

And fear is a liar. But a loud and convincing liar that can make it hard to hear anything besides his petty, mean-spirited voice. At the beginning of the most defining friendship humanity would ever be offered, fear yelled, "Hide!" and none of us have recovered:

> Then the man and his wife heard the sound of the LORD God as he was walking in the garden in the cool of the day, and they hid from the LORD God among the trees of the garden. But the Lord God called to the man, "Where are you?" He answered, "I heard you in

the garden, **and I was afraid** because I was naked; so I hid." (Gen. 3:8–10 NIV, emphasis mine)

Fear underlines every one of our insecurities with a grisly, pointed finger and tells us that we *are* our faults, our flaws, our sins. And then fear tries to erase us. And we are terribly eager to agree.

This is fear's endgame. To sever our ties to community. Because we were built for friendship.

"In the beginning was the Word, and the Word was with God, and the Word was God" (John 1:1). In the beginning. A perfect, triune friendship. Intimate. Safe. Beloved. Complete. And then God, out of the overflow of this full and satisfying relationship began the work of creation. And on the sixth day, God said, "Let Us make man in Our image, according to Our likeness. . . . So God created man in His own image; He created him in the image of God; He created them male and female" (Gen. 1:26–27).

And God breathed His own breath into us.

Into us God breathed the desire for companionship. Into us God breathed the gift of community. Into us God breathed all the capacity for believing the best about each other, loving others more than ourselves, and making ourselves wildly vulnerable without fear of betrayal.

Friendship was breathed into our DNA at the very beginning.

When I breathe in and out, there it is, right beneath my ribcage, the promise that I am capable of friendship, because my very existence—twenty breaths per minute—is drawn from the breath of the God, whose entire existence is a living, breathing fellowship of three.

Friendship was breathed into our DNA at the very beginning.

And fear wants to steal it back.

"The Devil delights in keeping people away from other people. He knows that the power of love is in relationship. And he is dedicated to our being cut off from God and each other."[2] So, instead of a quiet walk with a tender God, fear wants to send us on a frantic streak into hiding. We have since become experts at it. Fear is our loudest dictator. Friendship is terrifying because it's the place where fears can come true.

Fear of being hurt. Again. Fear of missing out, being left out, or feeling left out. Fear of being the new girl. Fear of including the new girl. Fear of being misunderstood, misinterpreted, and misfit. It's easy to understand why we women take one look at the friendship landscape pockmarked with an infinity of land mines and say, "Heck no!"

I won't dumb it down.

I won't pretend the potential for hurt isn't there. It is. Period. There are no guarantees when it comes to friendship. Except this one:

> There is no fear in love; instead, perfect love drives out fear.
> (1 John 4:18)

That's it. That's the choice. At the end of the day we get to choose who will have the final say in our lives and our relationships: fear or love.

I hope after you read this section, you'll recognize fear as a dead end, and love as the only choice that can fill us up. Fill us up so full there's plenty to spill over into the lives of the people around us. Into the lives of our friends.

THE FEAR OF BEING HURT. AGAIN. (FRIENDSHIP PTSD)

"Fact: Christian women will hurt you." —Mary[1]

WHOEVER SAID, "STICKS AND stones will break your bones, but words will never hurt you," must not have gone to junior high or been a woman. And while we might expect Christians to be the exception to this cruel rule, real life proves that they are not. "Anyone who has been in the church for very long has been hurt by people in the church."[2] Christians aren't immune to "judgment, pride, self-centeredness, manipulation, abandonment, abuse, control, perfectionism, domination, and every kind of relational sin known to humankind. The walls of the church do not make it safe from sin. In fact, the church by definition is composed of sinners."[3]

I've officially lost track of the number of stories I've heard from women who've been hurt by other women in ways that boggle the mind. Maybe we learn in girlhood how to invite and then disinvite a friend to our birthday party all in the same breath. My preschool daughter stunned me with that story this afternoon. With her wispy, baby breath I heard the words tumble out, "But then Sophie said I can't come to her birfday party anymore because I didn't play Fwozen with her on the playground today."

And I felt that terrible ache in my gut of something ancient beginning. Something so dark and ominous and seemingly inevitable that I wanted to stand Gandalf-like before it, blocking its way and bellowing, "You shall not pass!" But I know that I won't be able to bubble wrap her away from the world and all its sharp edges. So I want to be the one to equip her—to give her the courage and the tools to face the daunting statistics chronicling how we women treat each other.

That's why it's worth looking at the science behind our female craving for connection as well as some of the wounds surrounding the often-failed attempts for women to remain friends. We'll share personal stories of friendships failed and hurts survived by women just like us who chose to stay and try again. Because you're not alone in your fears. Not by a long shot.

Friendship PTSD

"The hardest breakup of my life was with a friend." —Annie[4]

My mom died one week to the day after I turned eighteen. And my first phone call after I got the news was to a girlfriend, Liza. I didn't even tell her what had happened. I didn't need to. I just asked if she could come and get me. Because she'd spent the last eighteen months keeping me company on the long, grueling journey of leukemia, hospices, learning to cook, and staying out too late to avoid going home to the cloud of sadness that hung over our home, she was no longer surprised by my requests. I didn't have my driver's license yet, and my dad was making phone call after phone call repeating the same terrible words over and over again. I wanted to get out of the house, out of range of that repeated disaster, out of my skin.

Liza's mom drove her over. And they took me back to their house. And I still didn't know how to break the news. Death is such an awkward conversation for teenage girls already awkward in their skinny jeans. But Liza did what she always did. She just let me be with her. She didn't expect anything from me. She fed me and shared her hair dye with me and played John Cougar Mellencamp loudly, and I could hide in plain sight because I felt safe in her bedroom knowing her mom would come in later and bring us tea or grilled hot dog sandwiches.

It was Dorothy who ended up breaking the news for me. We'd shared a classroom and church and youth group and too many hiking trips together to count since first grade, and there wasn't anything she didn't know about me. And as soon as her family got the news about my mom, Dorothy came looking for me. She had one foot in a cast and wasn't supposed to be driving, but she came limping up Liza's driveway with all my own sadness streaming down her face. She couldn't talk. Her grief was incoherent, and as soon as Liza's mom saw Dorothy, she came to find me and hold me, and I didn't have to put any of it into words—because that's what our friends do. Friends carry our sadness for us when we're terrified we'll be crushed under the weight of it.

One week before my life stopped, one week before I knew what it was like to be a motherless daughter, one week before I had to figure out a way to pronounce and swallow past the words, "My mom died," I was turning eighteen and thinking about prom and planning my dress with Bernadette and her mom. Where there were girlfriends, there was also the miracle of their mothers who loved me as their own and adopted me into their family traditions. After school and on the weekends when my dad was working, I always had a family to call my own even when mine was at its most fractured. And the day I turned eighteen, Bernadette's mom took me for a fitting of my prom dress. The midnight blue velvet fit like a glove that slipped on like a sigh after we'd had our hair and makeup done. Then Dad drove me to visit my mom at the hospice so I could show her the grown-up version of her daughter. The nearly eighteen-year-old woman who had no idea that it would be the first and last time her mother saw her baby girl as a woman, grown into her skin and her curves.

That night after I'd cried off my makeup and heard my mother call me beautiful and kissed her paper-thin cheek good night, I was at Bernadette's house for a birthday celebration recognizing my coming-of-age into my own womanhood. With gifts and laughter and more tears and so much generosity crammed around the dining room table, there was barely room for all my mixed-up feelings of delight and sorrow.

Rozanna was another living life preserver. And her family's townhouse, the place where there were no bad dreams, where we talked about our boy crushes and whispered our hopes for what growing up might feel like. Where we felt beautiful because her mom insisted we were, made us twirl in our new shoes, and then fed us comfort and Greek pastries.

There was also Vanessa and Gertrude. Adene, Melanie, and Xenia. For nearly two years my girlfriends cried all my tears, and when we were exhausted from the crying, they made me laugh and took me out for cappuccinos and never expected me to make conversation. They were my literal bones and marrow and sinew, holding me together so that I could figure out how to take another step forward when I'd forgotten how to breathe.

But what we didn't know is that grief is a very heavy thing to carry, and it sucks all the air out of a room until it suffocates even the brightest flame—and some friendships can't survive it.

Girls at eighteen are mesmerized by life. They need all the breath they can gulp down because there are so many stories waiting for them to inhale, waiting to wrap them up in wonder. So while I was living my own personal nightmare of a dead mother and a father who buried his grief in a hasty remarriage and then a painful divorce, my friends were growing into their own futures farther and farther away from mine. And it was inevitable that at some point they wouldn't want to carry my deadweight any further. They wouldn't be able to.

And so one night I was on the phone sharing the ridiculous, almost embarrassing drama that characterized my life the year after high school when one of them would call it quits. Would want out. Would want permission to let go of the weight of my grief that was drowning us both. And I understood. Because who wouldn't want to kick loose of that anchor and swim hard for the surface and great gulps of free air? I would have kicked free of it myself if I had the option.

But there it was. The breakup. And I stared at the phone and wasn't surprised but still there was a quiet trickle of blood from an internal injury that no one could see. You can bleed to death from broken friendships without ever telling anyone that it's happening. You can bleed from the loss of sharing the ordinary stories and secrets that make up the inner lives of girls. That's the magic of being invited into someone else's head. So when her door closes in your face and you're alone with your thoughts again, it's confusing even when it makes sense.

It will take you months to un-learn the habit of dialing her number, needing her opinion, wanting her company more than you want your own. "Neuroscience has discovered that our brain's very design makes it sociable, inexorably drawn into an intimate brain-to-brain linkup whenever we engage with another person."[5] So when that intimate link you've come to rely on as much as one of your own two legs is suddenly amputated, you'll trip and fall and forget over and over again that it isn't there to hold you up anymore.

We are wired to connect. As women, our craving for connection is so deep and our orientation toward attachment so primal that "we fear a rupture in relationship more than a loss of independence."[6] And every time we go through a friendship breakup, we're teaching our brains that friends can't be trusted. So the next time someone invites us through the door into their secret world, we're less likely to step through quite as trustingly as the first time. There's a reason little girls on the playground introduce themselves within seconds and mere minutes later declare themselves best friends, while their mothers watch from separate park benches.

A rupture in a relationship can feel like a bomb going off and can shake through every layer of your life, causing a kind of post-traumatic stress disorder (PTSD) in all future relationships. The fascinating field of social neuroscience explains why. In his book *Social Intelligence: The New Science of Human Relationships*, Daniel Goleman explains how every social interaction reshapes our brains through what is called "neuroplasticity." In other words, just like we learn not to touch that lighted candle after we get burned the first time, or how we might enjoy repeating the habit of late-night TV bingeing and ice cream, repeated social experiences teach us which relationships are hot to the touch and which ones are delicious. "By repeatedly driving our brain into a given register, our key relationships can gradually mold certain neural circuitry. In effect, being chronically hurt and angered, or being emotionally nourished, by someone we spend time with daily over the course of years can refashion our brain."[7]

First as little girls and then as teens and adults.

The patterns we live over and over again in our friendships aren't by accident. They're the actual rewiring of our brains to connect or not connect based on past experiences. So if we've had a defining relationship that ended up being a bomb that exploded in our hearts, we're more likely to experience some degree of post-traumatic stress when we find ourselves in a similar relationship situation in the future.

A problem emerges when we've become so programmed to expect the explosion that we start to see bombs where there aren't any anymore.

Sometimes that friendship bump you've run into isn't a bomb going off. Sometimes it's just the equivalent of a car backfiring in a friendship, but our brains have been so deeply wired to treat all conflict as explosive that we are quick to hide, to shut down, to reject first. We're trained to anticipate trouble where maybe there is none. Because we're protecting ourselves from hurt, we start to anticipate being hurt. When those kinds of life-altering explosions have rumbled through our childhoods, they are especially capable of causing seismic shifts well into our adult friendships without us ever realizing it.

Angela tells me that her daughter was "voted out" of her group of middle school girlfriends during lunch period one day.

Lisa shares how a decade after she was rejected, abandoned, and divorced by the husband she loved so much when first married, the ache is still raw and real.[8]

Becky has been hurt and watched her friends be hurt by church cliques.[9]

Tracey's mom never had friends due to the abuse from her dad, so Tracey doesn't know what's normal and what's not normal when it comes to friendship.[10]

I tripped over this discovery of how my early relationship experiences were still dictating my current friendships one afternoon when I was venting to my friend Janice about a friendship misunderstanding that had me twisted inside out. Instead of focusing on my current friendship frustration, she said, "Lisa-Jo, I think that there's a relationship bomb that went off in your life a long time ago. And that bomb is turning current friendship conflict into PTSD triggers."

She could see what I couldn't. She could see that my reaction to this current friendship conflict was way out of proportion. So we started to unpack it together because "our relationships have subtle, yet powerful, lifelong impacts on us."[11] This means that while they can burden us with unwelcome PTSD, they also have highly reparative capabilities too. The relationship patterns we have learned can become the clues that lead us back to the scene of the original crime and equip us with the tools to investigate, understand, and prevent it from happening again.

So on a Friday afternoon I set out to investigate where my friendship PTSD was originating. I've never thought of myself as a people pleaser, per se, but what I realized upon investigation is that I've become an expert people defuser. So much so that any conflict in the air I automatically set out to defuse. I own that conflict like it's directed at me and about me, and I absorb it and I hurt with it and my skin feels raw until I've managed to defuse it.

I constantly interpret someone's feelings about a situation as their feelings about me. When a friend is frustrated about something and they share that frustration with me, I'm quick to osmosis that into a sense of frustration directed at me. And as anyone knows, relationships are constantly going to be chock-full of all kinds of feelings, and if we constantly absorb those as our own, then we're swallowing a Molotov cocktail of our own concoction. And I was living with explosive insides that hurt every time someone else's stress or anger or frustration bumped up against me. Forget backfiring cars, all I could see was a minefield. And I took on the job of clearing and defusing it like a boss. The problem: that job was never supposed to be mine. Yours either, by the way.

When Janice lovingly told me that my reaction to regular, everyday friend stress was turning my insides into smoking cinders and that I needed to perhaps poke around to find out where the original bomb went off in my life, I was able to see my story in a way and from an angle I'd never imagined before.

Mapping Your Friendship DNA

My mom and dad were a classic case of opposites attracting. She described herself as the studious firstborn who grew up in a reserved Dutch family, well trained in the art of politely squelching their conflicts and their frustrations through sheer force of will and good manners. My dad, however, was the youngest by a decade, the spoiled last baby of his parents—his father having just returned from fighting in World War II, his mother a tough farmer's wife who ran the family estate in his absence with an iron fist and tea every afternoon at 4:00 p.m. To hear it told, my mom described the world he brought her into as loud and full of big, shouty feelings that no one ever considered not sharing. She said it was a relief. A shock, but it was a relief to meet my dad and his family because they lived all their feelings out loud.

My mom balanced my dad out. And our home growing up was one of big feelings—generous, passionate, loving ones. But sometimes, it was also a place where big angry feelings got out of control. Once my mom died and there was no counterbalance to my dad, I saw it as my firstborn duty to assume the role of the defuser. That's a lot for a teenager to own. That's shouldering adult baggage never intended for her. And turns out I've been carrying it ever since.

Until my friend Janice softly asked me what the bomb was that went off in my life. I looked back over my childhood and saw all the shrapnel of years spent living in the blast radius of a dying mother, a devastated father, two baby brothers, a shotgun remarriage, and the desperate attempt to put it all back together again. Or at least, to try to keep the peace. To say the right thing. To defuse.

I was ill equipped for it. A selfish teenager who mostly just wanted out. Who wanted to grow up into a different story and run away to another country for college. But I could never outrun the instinct to absorb the emotions around me as way of defusing them.

In case it's not already clear, that is not healthy. It's not healthy for an eighteen-year-old or a forty-one-year-old or a seventy-year-old. But old habits stick tight and it had never occurred to me that it might not be my job to keep the peace, to take the emotional temperature of every situation, and to try and fix it.

But on that fall Friday afternoon sitting in a puddle of sunshine on my bedroom floor, I finally saw that compulsion for what it was—someone else's baggage. I listened in on my eighteen-year-old self and saw all that she'd been expected to carry and then all that she'd foisted on her grown-up self. When I finally saw it, I could lovingly take that eighteen-year-old tenderly by the face and tell her it was okay to drop it. To just let all that emotional baggage she was trying to carry for someone else drop onto the floor, into the abyss, over the cliff's edge. She could drop it and she wouldn't implode. She wouldn't disappear into a million little bits of exploded stress.

Whatever the relationship baggage you're carrying on behalf of someone else, it's okay for you to drop it too. It's okay for you to stop taking all the weight of someone else's brokenness onto your own shoulders. Whether you inherited it from a parent, a sibling, or a friend. Whether it's people-pleasing or perfectionism, whether it's control or learned hiding or any of the devastating host of behaviors we learn in order to protect ourselves from hurtful relationships.

Some of you might be wondering, *But where do I even begin?* I can't speak for everyone, but I can share what worked for me. This is how I loosened my fists and released all that junk I didn't even know I'd been carrying around with me. I did a very simple exercise advised by my friend. I wrote myself two letters.

First little Lisa-Jo wrote a letter to big Lisa-Jo telling her about all that hurt. All the places the bomb had wounded her. All the ways she'd felt lonely and scared and misunderstood. I wrote it with my left hand. My baby hand. The hand that doesn't know how to hold a pencil properly. And so when I read it I could hear my younger self clearly through the purple marker and scrapbook paper.

And then I replied. I wrote myself back. My grown-up self wrote back using her right hand and her mature voice to reach in and answer the painful questions I'd been living in patterns of repeat for decades, without ever before pausing to see if they were healthy. So I pushed pause on that Friday afternoon and wrote back to myself explaining all the ways the various relationship bombs that had detonated throughout my childhood weren't my fault.

And we both cried—both parts of myself—and none of it was wasted because I knew the Holy Spirit was there writing the words and answering the questions with me and through me. Because He is a God who keeps track of all our sorrows. A God who collects all our hot tears in His bottle; who records each one in His book (Ps. 56:8). None of it was a surprise to Him. It was an act of freedom. Because "it is for freedom that Christ has set us free" (Gal. 5:1 NIV).

He wants to set you free too. So if you've stumbled around for years trying to make sense of why so many parts of friendship can still hurt, maybe you need to stop. Maybe you need to sit down. Maybe you need to figure out where the first relationship bomb went off in your life and take stock of the shrapnel and write yourself free. It's been both the hardest and simplest first step for me.

If you're reading this and you can feel your heart racing and hear the blood pounding in your ears, I think it's because you know there's something that was broken a long time ago, and for years you've thought it was your fault. There's some relationship that exploded in your life, and you've been re-living that trauma in ways you might not even have recognized every time you try to engage another woman in friendship.

Here's where that legacy ends. Jesus promises to set us free. He came in person, He moved into the neighborhood for the express purpose of staging a prison break—He wants you free from bondage. He wants to see you rise up on the wings of eagles. So if your eyes feel hot right now, and you need to dump your past onto paper, schedule some time to do it.

We must break the patterns that have defined our relationships and start to teach our brains new ones. If you did this exercise, read what you wrote. Read out loud what you wish you'd known to be true all those years ago. Or maybe it was just last month. Read and let it wash over you and set you free.

Forgiveness Is Ground Zero

Friends are hard work. Heck, people are hard work. There's no getting around it. The only way through is through. Through the knowing and the showing up and the forgiving and the laughing and the folding laundry together and the walking kids to school and the daring to do the ugly cry in front of each other.

Because there are no perfect people, inevitably someone will hurt us and we will hurt someone. What matters is what comes next. Will we forgive them, or will we withdraw? Will we work it out, or will we write it off? We are each broken and each wounded. But only by choosing to stay, can we start to grow deep roots. And forgiveness is always ground zero when it comes to any relationship, especially friendship.

I once heard the singer Ellie Holcomb say, "God didn't come to make bad people good; He came to make dead people alive." It rocked me because I think so much of our lives we spend trying to be good. We forget good is near impossible. It's life that Christ came to offer us. And only through His life offered for us can we ever arrive at the gift of goodness.

We are none of us bad or good; we are all of us dead. Dead in our sins and our old cycles of pain and lies and despair. And Jesus has come to breathe His own living breath into our dry bones. He calls your name into the tomb. He yells it. He sings it. He whispers it. He calls you by name in whatever way He knows you will hear Him best. And then He trades His own life for yours so that you can walk out of your past and your broken relationships and the shrapnel that has characterized your life and walk into the light to stand with Him—the greatest of all friends—beloved, whole, and heart-pumpingly alive.

But if we aren't able to leave our anger and bitterness and resentment in that tomb, it will snake out behind us like the rotting bandages of an undead mummy and wrap us up in knots. It will try to pull us back into the grave and make it impossible to walk forward into any kind of friendship with all of that still clawing at us.

The apostle Paul (formerly known as Saul before his conversion)—who so infamously hunted down the early Christians and personally signed their death warrants and witnessed their executions—understood this truth. He was haunted by his own legacy of sin and described it like this: "Wretched man that I am! Who will deliver me from this body of death?" (Rom. 7:24 ESV).

Paul's question is much more gruesome than it appears on the surface. He may have been referencing one of the Roman Empire's more torturous forms of executing justice—the practice of strapping the corpse of a murder victim to the back of the murderer.[12] Under penalty of death, no one was allowed to liberate the condemned person.[13] And ultimately the death and decay from the rotting corpse—the body of death—would make its way into the living person, infecting every cell and organ until they died in a way that makes all our zombie, vampire, and undead franchises pale in comparison.

Paul literally felt the weight of his own sin and his inability to live up to God's law like a dead body dragging him down with it. I know what that feels like. I'm guessing you do too. Because Satan would like nothing more than to see all of us women infected by our past hurts, the lies we've believed, and the grievances we bear. If it were up to him he would strap the corpses of our failed friendships and dead relationships to our backs and have us carry them into every conversation, every tender connection, and new interaction. Into every Bible study and book club, into every girls' night out and kids' birthday party.

But Jesus says, "I have come that they may have life, and have it to the full" (John 10:10 NIV). He's the only one who can cut that dead weight of broken relationships and old patterns off our backs. The only one who can holler our names and invite us into community with Him and set us free to embrace friendship, connection, and vulnerability. Life—He has come to offer us His own life so that we can have our own lives back. He wants us to have all that He knows to be true about community—that it is good, so very good.

Forgiveness is ground zero. Forgiveness is where we begin. Forgiveness is walking out of the tomb of our own making. Forgiveness is no to death and yes to life. Forgiveness is all that we've been given—passing it on to someone else. Without forgiveness, friendship becomes extinct and relationship nonexistent. In his book about the new science of human relationships, Daniel Goleman calls forgiveness "an antidote" to the "lasting biological consequences" of cycles of rage, hurt, and revenge.[14] Forgiving someone who has hurt us actually reverses those biological reactions: "It lowers our blood pressure, heart rate, and levels of stress hormones and it lessens our pain and depression."[15]

Without forgiveness, friendship becomes extinct and relationship nonexistent.

In my own experience there's something of a sliding scale for how hard it will be to forgive someone. On the one end of the scale are the people who hurt us unwittingly. They didn't plan to hurt us. They hurt us by accident, by being careless with our feelings, or completely ignorant of what the impact of their actions were. These are the people we trust and that deep down in our gut we know are rooting for our best. And knowing that they never meant to hurt us goes a long way in helping us forgive them.[16]

But on the other end of that sliding scale is a dark and wretched place—because there lie the hurts caused by people on purpose. Or by people who were so cavalier with our hearts that even if we tried to show them our open wounds, they'd shrug their shoulders and go back to their coffee.

Beth Moore describes in wrenching words the exact feelings I've had in those situations: "How often have I made a fool of myself just trying to get someone who hurt me to hear me?"[17] The deep injustice of being wounded by someone who doesn't care or isn't interested in understanding our pain can feel like acid burning away your skin. You feel stripped emotionally bare, skin raw and flaming with the unfairness of it all.

On the day I was baptized, I had someone walk up to me and hand me a card. And what I thought was going to be a note full of love and affirmation and finally reconciliation from someone who had haunted my life with misery for months turned out to be a blistering screed of condemnation and ugliness. Handed to me in church. On the day I was publicly dedicating my life to the Lord. Twenty years later I can still feel the impact of that slap.

On the day Joseph was sent out to check on his brothers and bring them word from their father, their hatred boiled over while he was still at a distance. It then grew hands and fingers that stripped off his technicolor dreamcoat the moment he arrived and threw him into a deep gash in the earth. After plotting the death of their little brother, they casually "sat down to eat a meal" (Gen. 37:25). Beth Moore hauntingly describes the scene: "Genesis 42:21 describes what was emanating from the pit while the brothers had their picnic. The Amplified Bible says it best: 'We saw the distress and anguish of his soul when he begged us [to let him go], and we would not hear.'"[18]

The terrible injustice of people in your life who move from hurting you to dishing up supper without ever taking a breath in between to say they're sorry can make you want to vomit. It's a relief to know I'm not the only one who feels this way. It's why I run to reading Beth Moore when I need to remember that forgiveness is possible every time I'm tempted to hold a deep and satisfying grudge. Because her life aches with the kind of hurt and child abuse I can't wrap my mind around forgiving. She doesn't try to sell us on it being easy. She wants us to know it will be *necessary*. And ultimately it will be more satisfying than revenge. Because "forgiveness is not passivity, dear one. It is power. It is the ability to withstand the pressing, quaking gates of hell. Take this power and wield it. It's your right as a child of God. In the power of Jesus, first you will it and soon you'll feel it."[19]

But how? How do we grope our way to forgiveness? Not because we want to or even because we're capable. But only because there are giant footprints we can sink our desperate feet into. We can walk in the shoes of Christ because He did it first. He forgave. While being tortured, He looked out into the faces of His torturers and He said the immortal words, "Father, forgive them, for they do not know what they are doing" (Luke 23:34).

This is only possible because "Forgiveness is not about feeling. It's about willing. No stronger force exists. Forgiveness was the force that kept Christ, by His own submission, nailed to that cross. He could have taken Himself down in a split second. He could have called upon every archangel in the heavens, armed and ready. Had He said the word, the seas would have swallowed the earth in one gulp."[20]

But instead He chose to forgive them because He knew that they didn't have a clue. "Whoever threw you into the pit doesn't have any idea how much it hurt you. I'm not sure they would get it even if you told them in detail upon detail. No, they don't have a clue how much it affected your decisions and relationships. Humbly, but very specifically, forgive them not only for their destructive actions, but also for their ignorance. You have no other choice if you want out of that pit."[21]

And that's what we want, yes? Out of the pit. Out of the tomb. Out of the gaping maw of death that would like nothing more than to close its jaws around us and suck us down. But we were made for life, and God wants to give us life—life to the full. The kind of life that isn't smothered by mummified hatred passed down from one generation to the next. There's only one way to hack away at that darkness. It's the blazing sword of forgiveness.

Nothing takes "more divine power than forgiveness, and therefore nothing [is] more powerful than forgiving."[22] But forgiveness doesn't necessarily imply friendship, however. "Forgiveness does not require condoning some offensive act, forgetting what happened, or reconciling with the perpetrator. It means finding a way to free oneself from the claws of obsession about the hurt."[23] Forgiveness is making peace with the past so that there is opportunity for relationship in the future. Not necessarily with the same people who've scarred us. But sometimes, by the grace of Christ, forgiveness is exactly that powerful to restore broken relationships to fresh health and offer the same people a completely different way of relating to one another.

Twenty-three years after my mom's death, my father is a completely different person. And our relationship is a beautiful, healthy, breathing thing that has healed and restored and made us both new. So much of who we both were had to die and then be raised to life in Christ. And I often tell him now that if I weren't a believer, his metamorphosis alone would be proof enough for me that there is a God who cares about our lives enough to change us from the inside out. Remarried to a woman we love and esteem and with three adopted kids almost the same ages as my own, my dad is now one of the most significant role models in my life; he consistently models what grace, patience, and compassion look like when lavished into the lives of children.

Forgiveness is the beginning. And it's how we find closure even in the relationships that won't ever be completely restored to us. Because forgiveness is like a pair of tweezers picking out the shards of shrapnel embedded in our hearts and minds by people we once loved. Forgiveness removes the hurt so that we can heal. Forgiveness is the gift we give to ourselves so that we can stop bleeding and begin to grow new skin over old wounds. Forgiveness is the first step out of the dark and into the light.

THE FEAR OF MISSING OUT
(FOMO)

*"The enemy loves him some lonely women, and he'll
settle for us feeling alone and left out even if nothing
could be further from the truth." —Kristen*[1]

THE INTERNET HAS COMPLICATED our relationships with an already complicated fear—the fear of missing out or being left out, the fear of being excluded, rejected, or ignored. On purpose. Because while decades ago we might have been the last person picked for the dance squad, debate team, art project, or sleepover, at least the only people who would have known or cared enough to comment on it were limited to the people who actually knew us in real life. And unless someone told us to our face, we were most likely blissfully unaware about who went where and did what over the weekend or what event was happening two schools over that we weren't invited to.

Not so today. The Internet allows us to zoom in on the lives of friends and strangers alike until we're nose to nose with what we missed, who didn't invite us, and how much fun happened without us. This fear has the grisly honor of having been elevated to pop cult status and awarded its own online acronym—FOMO—or Fear of Missing Out.

Add to that the fact that the Internet has also opened up whole new super highways of opportunities for us to covet our neighbor's life, bookshelves, paint colors, parenting, messy bun, exercise stats, vacation, kitchen, or college experience. And it's a twenty-car pileup with very few making it out unscathed.

So let's unpack the family of fears that live under this giant rock called Missing Out. And in the process help us put those fears into their proper perspective.

The Fear of Missing Out—FOMO

"We don't have a word for the opposite of loneliness, but if we did, I could say that's what I want in life." —Marina Keegan[2]

I think it's what we all want. Not to feel lonely. To live a life full of the opposite of loneliness. We want welcome and closeness and connection and invites for hot chocolate and evenings spent catching up and mornings that warm us with the leftover glow from time spent with people who love us.

We want to be seen.

But we live in a world saturated by images with a million different stories and faces and Instagram accounts and Facebook pages and Pinterest boards and Snapchats all competing for the same real estate—to rise to the surface of what catches the eye.

A million people longing to be seen.

So many images to choose from. So many stories of togetherness. And all of them flitting past us like so many window displays. *Look at that pretty table! Look at what fun they had at the beach! Look at those women worshipping together, or book clubbing together, or biking together.*

And we awkwardly bear witness to a thousand other lives all from the other side of the window. The *outside.* It can crush a heart. It can make a soul feel empty, uninvited, unwelcome.

If we let it.

A few summers back we spent six days in northern Michigan lake country with no Internet, cell, or data connection.

No suffocating sense of loneliness, competition, or comparison either. No dread at seeing that photo of that thing you weren't invited to join.

It gets a girl thinking real hard about this online space where we all spend so much time. And wondering how to carve out quiet, safe spaces for the soul to remember it is beloved, pursued, cherished, and called in the midst of the chaos we wade through every day.

The sky was so big and the water so wide it made me feel small in all the right ways.

Not because my house is too small or my wardrobe too limited or my tool-box of skills too worthless or my online presence too tiny compared to someone else's. No, it made me feel small because that's the appropriate reaction for a human being to have when she tilts her head back and gets a glimpse of the God who sculpted all that awesome with His bare hands.

The horizon that aches on forever and the tiny minnows that dart and dash between my sons' toes. How the same God breathed life into both. The daunting expanse of the cosmos stretched out above us like a hammock and the sand sifted and squished beneath our bare feet.

I am so small in that context. And it's a relief.

We were not built for big.

We were built to reflect the glory of the God who is big. And who is not afraid to speak to us in a still, small voice; a gentle whisper. "And after the earthquake a fire, but the Lord was not in the fire; and after the fire [a sound of gentle stillness and] a still, small voice" (1 Kings 19:12 AMP).

And I heard it as I kicked the swing back and forth, back and forth at the side of Little Traverse Lake with the water gently lapping up to the rock levy. Aunt Marcia sat next to baby Zoe and me. Zoe held on to her face with both hands and they were both laughing. Aunt Marcia who had been fighting tumors in her lungs and brain for the past year and who kept showing up in real life. I could see her because I'd slowed down enough to stop looking past everything that was right in front of me.

But, before that, on the long drive from Virginia to Michigan and then up into the palm of the mitten to Peter's family's lake cabin, I was still tracking everyone online—tracking their vacation plans from my thumb on the front seat of the minivan, flicking through photo after photo.

Then once we hit Traverse City I couldn't get any kind of reception on my phone. No text messages or Facebook or Instagram or Twitter. No blog posts or Pinterest or glimpses into what other people were doing that didn't include me. No ache from the annual event that never has my name on the list but, nonetheless, floods my Internet feeds with updates and prayers and faces reflecting all the wonder of being invited.

Instead, all I heard in that quiet moment in Michigan was the lapping lake and Aunt Marcia holding my baby girl, giggling at her over the rims of her sunglasses as a speedboat chugged by in the distance and someone lazily called out for a refill on their drink.

Not having access to people's lives a thousand miles away focused all my attention on the lives of the people right in front of me. The miracle of their lives lived in between an aunt's cancer and a baby girl's first swim in the lake and all of it the reflected glory of the God who calls them both by name and knows each beat of their hearts from the inside out. The God who gave them to me and me to them and calls us all family.

Later that week, there was an afternoon we all sat out on the front yard of Uncle David and Aunt Marcia's farm and watched the cousins play soccer. Then Aunt Marcia surprised us by getting up from her seat and sprinting into the game, laughing and keeping up with the boys. Her mom and her sister and nieces cheered from the sidelines, tired from late nights of catching up and fireworks and little boys racing around with their big cousins and uncle on the Gator. And when she sat back down next to me laughing and sweating and so wholly alive, I took her photo. I asked if I could share it sometime and she said, "Yes! Go tell them how I fought and how I made it and how I'm here today."

I've carried her words in my mind, and I've been the only one to read them for a long time. Because that summer day in Michigan there was no way to post them because the Internet had slipped out of reach of my fingers and my phone had run out of battery from neglect. More importantly I'd remembered what it feels like to belong in the spaces where we were made to fit. Instead of the ones we only wish we could fit into.

It makes me simultaneously want to quit the Internet and forge deep into it to grab Christ's daughters by the shoulders and shake them and repeat real loud into their beautiful eyes, "You are chosen, wanted, necessary, lavishly loved. There is only one you, and we need you not to disappear, duck, hide, or give up to the lie that you don't belong."

We need you here and now. We need you to fight your way through so that you can look around at your family, at your people, and say, "Yes, I made it and I'm here today." You are necessary. You are not invisible. You are named and seen, and please don't erase your relevance because you think you're not relevant to the people you pass by on a screen.

Social media has turned all of us to some degree or another into Peeping Toms who spend hours of every day watching from the outside of the window what's happening inside the lives of people we know and often people we don't. And what we want and what we experience morph into two very different sides of the same coin—we want connection, but what we experience instead is loneliness.

You are necessary. You are not invisible. You are named and seen, and please don't erase your relevance because you think you're not relevant to the people you pass by on a screen.

David Kinnaman, president of The Barna Group, describes it like this: "As a nation, we are embracing the digital revolution and, ironically, we are becoming a lonelier population. While there are many benefits of being participants in possibly the most relationally connected age in human history, the social media revolution has *not* made us feel more connected, less lonely, or replete with friends."[3]

Or in the words of social media user Kathy,[4] "I think behind our Internet communication are many, many women craving one-on-one, face-to-face time with each other. I know the Internet, family, work take up much of my time. I've neglected friends and in a way gave up on new friendship. I don't like it. I want closer friendship again."

This is a rising trend. We are all craving closer friendship. Barna Group confirms, "While loneliness among Americans has risen, the desire to find one's place among a few good friends has likewise increased—from 31% a decade ago to 37% today."[5]

How do we do it, though?

How do we find our way into the places of being wanted and necessary and befriended?

How do we unlearn the lie that we've been left out on purpose? That we weren't good enough to include? That someone is more beloved than we are? How do we speak truth to the fear of missing out?

I don't think it's as simple as turning social media off.

The roots of the lie that we've been left out on purpose run deep and need to be dug up with a deliberate and single-minded mission. Because it's an ancient lie that's been growing in the heart of humanity since Adam and Eve first believed in the garden that God was holding out on them, excluding them from being like God, from knowing good and evil (Gen. 3:4–5).

We need to tear up the roots of that lie perpetrated on us. The lie that grows and curls its python-like vines around our lonely hearts and squeezes out any hope of believing that we belong. We need to hack away at the coils that are wrapped around our minds so that we aren't trapped by the four walls of an Instagram photo; so that we understand that God is always about invitation, about meeting us out in the "wide open spaces of God's grace and glory" (Rom. 5:2 MSG). Spaces that never fill up, that don't have a maximum capacity, that aren't designed for limits but instead, created to generously pour more and more and more into our lives than we could ever possibly cup in just two hands.

To decapitate the lie of being left out, we need to find its head. And if I pried open my heart, I believe I'd find two venomous fangs buried deep in that soft tissue pumping all the poison of a lifetime of the same message in a million different versions—the message that I have been left out on purpose—into my blood stream and around my body with a vengeance.

I am in desperate need of an antidote when I can't trust my own heart.

This is not a secret, and it shouldn't be a surprise. The ancient prophet, Jeremiah wrote, "The heart is more deceitful than anything else" (Jer. 17:9). There is no one better at lying to ourselves than ourselves. How many times have you opened Facebook or Instagram only to catch a glimpse of an event you didn't know was happening in your town and that you weren't invited to? Or that a friend was in the area and didn't ever reach out to you? How many times have we translated those images into the assumption that it was done on purpose? That the failure to connect or invite or include was because we were somehow found lacking? How often have we jumped from a photograph to a full-page story in our own heads that stars us as the excluded victim?

But God is a heart-knower, and He can liberate us from our hearts poisoned by the enemy's lies. "I the LORD search the heart and examine the mind" (Jer. 17:10 NIV).

The great doctor, the great healer, the tender psychologist has the antidote to the lies we believe if we'll only let Him treat us. David—the shepherd, the youngest of seven sons, the poet and king, the musician, and the worrier like you and me—wrote, "You delight in truth in the inward being, and you teach me wisdom in the secret heart" (Ps. 51:6 ESV). Jesus, "the way, the truth, and the life" (John 14:6) is the only One who can open up your secret heart and gently extract the fangs of poison that are lodged there. The only One who can decapitate the lie wrapped tight around our poor, gasping hearts. He has promised that He will and we can hold Him to it: "I will give you a new heart and put a new spirit within you; I will remove your heart of stone and give you a heart of flesh" (Ezek. 36:26).

Jesus will deliver us from the venom of our enemy.

Jesus is the only One who can give us hearts of truth, hearts of flesh, hearts that aren't poisoned beyond recognition by the lie of having been left out. Hearts that He calls by name and that believe they are seen.

But first comes the heart transplant. And heart transplants are delicate procedures.

As a medical resident in Cape Town, my father studied under Dr. Christiaan Barnard who became the first doctor in the world to successfully perform a human heart transplant on December 3, 1967. The operation lasted nine hours and used a team of thirty people. I wish I could tell you my dad was there for it. But he wasn't. He was there for the long, tedious months of preparation it took to pull off that surgery.

My dad is a fantastic storyteller. And as he tells it in his enthusiastic South African accent, the pork board of South Africa had offered Dr. Barnard an unlimited supply of pigs to practice the procedure. As kids, our eyes would get big as he described how they'd have an anesthetized pig open on the operating table, heart beating and waiting for the transplant. Then the smallest detail would go wrong and the heart would flatline, forcing them to begin again.

Over and over again. Until Louis Washkansky, a fifty-four-year-old grocer suffering from incurable heart disease, was desperate enough to offer himself as the first human patient. Dr. Barnard later wrote, "For a dying man it is not a difficult decision because he knows he is at the end. If a lion chases you to the bank of a river filled with crocodiles, you will leap into the water, convinced you have a chance to swim to the other side."[6]

But as desperate and courageous as their patients were, many surgeons couldn't stomach cardiac transplantation because of the consistently poor results, often due to rejection of the transplanted heart by the patient's immune system.[7] Dr. Barnard's first successful heart transplant patient only lived eighteen days before succumbing to pneumonia.[8]

But when we are desperate enough to live, we will take our chances swimming with the crocodiles. When we need to escape the lies that chase us, we might finally be prepared to risk everything. When we need the truth about our own acceptance. When our breath is raspy and gaspy from trying to live on a heart pumping the toxic lies of our own existence and our perceived exclusion through our bodies, we will finally come to Christ and ask Him to remove the heart that is twisting us into a version of ourselves we can't face in the mirror.

And He will.

He will rip His own bloody and still-beating heart out of His chest and graft it into ours. He will give us all of Himself to give us a chance at life. Desperate. Daring. And then the waiting will begin. To see if the new heart will take or if we'll reject it.

And Christ, the greatest heart surgeon, will give us the balm of the Holy Spirit to oversee the grafting process. But ultimately, what we bring into that holy sanctuary of our new beating heart will determine if it lives or if we die. Tim Keller teaches that what we put in our "Hallowed Place" is what will define us. Remember that line from the Lord's Prayer? "When we say, 'Hallowed be Thy name,' we are making the adoration of God the ultimate concern of our lives. By giving God the praise He deserves, we will heal our worldview as well as our souls."[9]

In other words, if we want our living hearts to survive the transplant, we have *got* to demote our social media status, our obsession with inclusion, and our fear of missing out and get it OUT of the hallowed place. We have worshipped at the altar of inclusion when we were built to worship at the altar of the only living God.

Living tied to clicks and likes and friend requests on Facebook will drain the life out of us.

> ## We have worshipped at the altar of inclusion when we were built to worship at the altar of the only living God.

But our hearts will easily beat in time to the holy rhythm that hallows God over and above everything else, especially ourselves, because it's what we were built for—to glorify God and enjoy Him forever.[10]

So when the Savior decapitates the lying serpent, pries its fangs from our hearts, and grafts His own holy, delighted, others-centered organ into our bodies, we will outlive the lie that we have been left out. Because now our internal compass will be pointing us back to the promise that we were always planned and wanted and included from before the beginning of time. The drumbeat of God's love and acceptance will beat in our very chests and echo in our ears and reverberate around our lives.

As the new heart does its work, pumping life and truth through us, hurt from exclusion will be drowned out by a new message—that while it may have hurt when you didn't get that invite to what "everyone else is doing. It feels so good to finally realize you are good enough and worthy *even without the invite*" —Alecia, (in)courage blog reader.[11]

37

THE FEAR OF BEING (OR INCLUDING) THE NEW GIRL

"Recently my daughter started a new school and I have never felt so alone during the gatherings that involve the other parents. They already have their friendships formed, their groups, and a few of them have come up to me to say hello, yes. But, after the casual pleasantries they go to their groups and I am left to my own devices. Usually at that point I just get on my cell and act as if I have lots to do. Lots of checking Facebook and email. LOL. How sad is that?" —Jennifer[1]

THE THING ABOUT WOMEN is that we always assume the girl next door, the woman across the aisle, the mom in the car pool lane, your husband's best friend's wife, your cousin, great-aunt, or the stranger in the dressing room next to you at the mall has it all figured out.

Whether "it" is how to manage her temper or style her hair or stock her fridge or connect with her husband or balance motherhood with the rest of life.

We're always certain we're the only one who feels awkward or incompetent or left out or frumpy or you-name-it. When it comes to making friends, that assumption can sideline us for years. Take it from me. I know.

For nearly two years after we moved to Virginia, I assumed that all the other women at church knew each other. I assumed I was the only newbie and that I was the only one who felt squirmy awkward in her skin during, what is to my mind, the worst ten minutes of church. If you grew up in a church or go to church or have even just popped your head into a church on Easter or Christmas, then you know what I mean. I'm talking about the ten minutes that can make an introvert want to crawl out of her skin. The well-intended opportunity to greet the folks around you. Some churches call this the "passing of the peace." Others call it the "meet and greet" or "fellowship" time. And if you're still not sure what I mean, kindly imagine yourself in any social setting where you are forced to endure that most dreaded ritual, the "ice breaker."

I'm a church lifer. I was born to parents who were working as missionaries, so church was pretty much one of my first languages. But to this day I still feel a growing sense of dread the nearer we get to the meet-and-greet portion of the service. I just can't even when it comes to turning around to the sweet folks in the pew behind me. The handshaking and trying to remember people's names and inevitably forgetting (again) and the brief chance to try and cram something from your week into a few awkward sentences. Just all of it—it's all excruciating.

I try to spend as much time as possible "greeting" my husband and kids (if they happen to be in the service with us instead of in Sunday school) so that I'm spared the awkwardness of trying to have a whole conversation without saying the name of the darling grandma behind me because I still can't seem to get my miserable brain to remember names more than thirty seconds after someone says them to me.

Once I'm through it, I'm always relieved and sometimes I'm a little bit happy that I got to meet sweet Bea from Ghana or Miriam from the military family who has kids the same ages as mine. But mostly I'm just grateful it's over, and I can go back to sitting without talking to anyone. Especially as the mother of a daughter. Getting to sit for an hour without answering a question or listening to a barrage of information is an incredible relief.

So for two years in Virginia the meet and greet was my nemesis. I didn't know anyone beyond (sometimes) remembering a first name and repeating the same information week after week ("Yes, it was a good week. Yes, the kids are growing so fast, thanks.") Until one day I sort of thought God might be nudging me to do something about it.

But first, I resisted for a good long time.

I had received a Bible study leader's kit in the mail as a marketing promotion, and I promptly put it under my desk and started using it as a footstool. True story. It was exactly the right height I needed to make my awkward desk and uncomfortable chair a tad more sit-able for long periods of time. For weeks I sat with my feet resting up on that Bible study leader's kit. Not once during that time did it occur to me that I might actually, you know, *use it.*

But then one Sunday after church, I was horrified to find myself walking up to Laura, who sat a few rows in front of me, and asking her if she'd be interested in joining a Bible study. The week before she'd mentioned in passing (I think it might even have been during the dreaded meet and greet) that she was looking for women mentors in her life. I guess it stuck with me. Because suddenly as the service was ending I had a vivid picture of that Bible study kit and Laura's comment: and before I knew it I was actually initiating a conversation and she was actually responding.

I was even more horrified when she said yes.

It went downhill from there. Laura insisted on telling other people about what I'd hoped would be a very, very small group. And other women wanted to join. Instead of the tiny, almost non-group I'd hoped for, the first night about seventeen women arrived. Even then, even as the person with the Bible study kit who'd initiated the invitation, I was sure they all knew each other and even though I was leading I'd still manage to be the odd one out.

And then we introduced ourselves.

There were women in that circle who'd been coming to the same church for decades without ever making a close friend.

There were women with daughters who were hurting themselves.

There were women who felt useless and lonely.

There were women who taught me the term *banshee mama* and could relate to what I thought was my solitary struggle with temper, frustration, and the sheer lunacy of the toddler-hard days.

There were women who felt like they didn't fit.

There were women who were sure all the other women already knew each other.

I cannot possibly overstate my surprise. And my regret that it took me so long to get my feet off that Bible study kit and use it as a way to walk into the lives of all the women who'd been showing up around me the past two years of Sunday mornings.

Every other Tuesday we would meet and share. We showed up in our sweats or our suits or our jeans and we talked. Some of us came straight from work, some from long days of homeschooling, or others were simply relieved for a chance to get out of their silent, empty apartments and find company for a couple of hours. It wasn't always profound. But we just kept showing up. We called ourselves the Tuesday night girls. And over and over again we had conversations that disproved the prejudice that we are each somehow on the outside looking in. Because when you tell your stories, you start to recognize yourself in the stories of others. You start to discover that you are both, in fact, inside a shared story.

Eventually we finished that Bible study kit, but we decided that the best part had been the showing up and the connecting. So we kept right on meeting. Every other Tuesday night at a local coffee shop. Whoever arrived first would grab a big table and women would trickle in as their schedule allowed. Sometimes almost all of us showed up and sometimes just a handful. Sometimes we stayed so late that the grumpy night janitor would give us the stink eye from under grim eyebrows and smack his vacuum cleaner against our chairs to make his point. We'd skedaddle out of there like giggling teenagers.

Turns out, every woman has days or years when she feels like the new girl.

It was the most educational experience I've had as a grown woman when it comes to figuring out friendship. Turns out, every woman has days or years when she feels like the new girl. No matter how long we might have been at that church or that school or that camp, there's a new girl in each of us as we constantly try to navigate new situations that arise and new decisions we have to make and new people we meet, and it can paralyze the most outgoing of us.

I like how Tricia, an (in)courage blog reader, sums it up:

It's hard being the "newbie." You look around and see all the circles of friendships and wonder how you are going to jump in. That's when your insecurities start messing with you and that's when you retreat, run, grow bitter, and quit. It takes courage, only from Christ, to give us strength to step out of our comfort zone. I am in this exact season. My family has been visiting a new church and there are friendships that are seasoned, but I have to continue to remind myself that we are not the only new ones. There are other women, moms, and wives that feel the same way I do. I just need to pray that God in His glorious assigning crosses our paths![2]

I find that newness only gets worn away by being willing to bump up against the nitty-gritty parts of someone else's life. Politeness will only get us so far. A ten-minute "meet and greet" during a church service won't even scratch the surface of trying to get to know someone. Any attempt to really connect is, inevitably, going to start by hauling us out of our comfort zones and into that place where we actually have to do the weird dance of asking for a phone number or e-mail address if we actually want to learn more than each other's first names.

I'm so done assuming that all women know all the other women in my social circles. The thing is, there's always room for one more friend and room to know each other more. Better. Deeper. Uglier. Weirder. Funnier. For better or worse, female friendships take courage to start and courage to maintain. Looking back now, I'm horrified at the friendships I might have missed if I'd remained hung up on being the new girl.

We moved to Maryland this past summer, and one of the hardest parts was the loss of my Tuesday night girls. The loss of seven years invested in their community and friendship in one consistent neighborhood. Often, I have to remind myself to stop whining about it all and to start over. I have to remind myself that my best friend and neighbor, Lisa, didn't always used to just swing by my house for tea and time to catch up in between work and the kindergarten pickup line. She started out as that mom who looked like she had it all together. That mom who was on the PTA, who ran the special arts appreciation program, who hosted beautiful birthday parties, and who knew all the other teachers and parents by first and last name. That kind of mom who used to intimidate me to death and didn't look like she needed one more friend. But after my son came home talking about how her daughter had told him where to sit in gym and kept turning up as the highlight of all his new friend stories, I took the chance during back-to-school night and mentioned how grateful I was for her daughter. And then I gave her my number.

Seven years later Lisa's number is still in my phone under her daughter's name. And Lisa is still my first phone call. No matter what. Sprained ankles, lice, a new writing project, family drama, or that new chick flick. I call Lisa.

Now, sure, there have been many, many other attempts with other women who've been too busy or too overwhelmed or whatever other "too" might be taking up space in their lives that left no real room to connect. And that's okay. Because it only takes one. It only takes one friend to fill us up and pull us out of our phobias about being "new." One friend will kryptonite-proof you against that paranoia that you don't belong. One friend will insulate you with the delicious sense of familiarity in a completely unfamiliar group. Lisa was my one over and over and over again for those seven years, and it was hard thinking about doing it again without her. But because I remembered how it started, I had a head start on knowing how to start over. Back to basics. The shortest distance between strangers is often a shared honest story. Or kids in the same grade. Or on the same baseball team.

As I transitioned to life in Maryland, I remembered Lisa, but I also remembered Bobbi. And remembering Bobbi was the urgent reminder not to wait too long before making the first move to connect with another woman.

Bobbi is much younger than I am, has four kids, and is (in my opinion) much cooler than I am. We both attended every baseball game for an entire season while our kids' team flailed to figure out batting and fielding. She seemed to manage her tribe of tiny humans effortlessly, while I hauled my crew around by the scruff of their whiny necks. Bobbi would hand out a creative assortment of snacks as she kicked around in her sneakers and jeans and ponytail that looked like they still belonged in college, not the major leagues of parenting four kids under the age of six. She seemed unflappable and totally fun and, while we had friends in common, I didn't know how to get to know her.

She was new to the neighborhood and seemed to instantly fit. I would see her at the playground and the ballgame and the pool that summer and felt lame and old and tired and uncool around her. Even though I had that familiar tug in my gut to just go ahead already and connect with her, the awkward teenager inside me preferred to hang back and smile and nod and leave it at that. This time Bobbi was the new girl—they'd relocated for her husband's job. But I couldn't seem to find a way to casually include her that didn't make me feel awkward. Yeah, focusing on yourself and your own insecurities instead of the mom who's new to the neighborhood? That was such a dumb choice.

One afternoon before we had to pick our kids up at school, Bobbi swung by my house to get something—I don't even remember what it was or which mutual friend prompted her asking if it would be okay to run by my place to get it. But she did. And then we sat at the sticky dining room table, the one with the paint stains and marker scribbles from a decade of kids coloring there, and we talked about all the things I didn't know.

I didn't know how hard it had been adjusting to northern Virginia after life in California. I didn't know the ridiculous challenges that had sprouted all over their rental house. I didn't know how lonely she was or how much she wished we'd had a chance to connect months before. I didn't know because I was so worried about being the "uncool girl" to her "new girl" that I forgot the cardinal rule of friendship: you have to be willing to go first.

And when Bobbi and I finally took that step, and laughed over the quirks of our kids, and compared parenting notes, and ate Pho together, I was immediately hit with a ton of regret that I'd left it so late. That I'd waited so long to try and get to know this wonderful woman with her awesome ability to be so present and interested in your life and to so delightfully welcome you into hers. All those baseball games wasted. All those poolside afternoons lost.

The cardinal rule of friendship: you have to be willing to go first.

One of my last months in town, she came with me to a speaking event, and she was there in the car as I was having a silent panic attack over the thought of walking into that building and encouraging other women while my own home front seemed so ridiculously chaotic. Before I knew it, she was asking if it would be okay if she prayed with me. I was so grateful. Relief rolled over me like a warm tide as Bobbi prayed. And the stress uncramped around my heart, and I could walk into the building and laugh into the eyes of the women. I could be 100 percent my real true, messy self because Bobbi had been there to remind me what that looked like. Because she knew. Because I'd finally invited her in.

That night I was so mad at myself that I'd waited so long to become friends with Bobbi. I'd let my stupid insecurity about what she might say if I tried to invite her into our neighborhood community trump the fun it seemed like it would be to get to know her. I mean, what's the worst that can happen? A new girl or mom or student moves onto your street or dorm room floor and you invite her out to a movie or a shopping trip and she says no? That's it. That's about the whole worst that can go down. She can say no, and she can stay home, and she can choose not to engage your community. You still have your friends. You haven't lost anything. But, if she says yes, if she's a new voice, if she has a wild laugh, if she's willing to share her grandma's recipe for blueberry soufflé or come over on the days your kids are rotating through the worst of the latest stomach bugs and drop off dinner? That friend, that's the friend you'll never regret having reached out to.

Bobbi and Lisa. The Tuesday night girls. These women became the reason that the meet-and-greet time during church began to lose its awkwardness. Because, for the first time in years of attending the same church, I now had women I was dying to snatch a moment with for a quick word. And let's get real here, there's no such thing as "a quick word" between women. So often our "meet and greet" would relocate into the hallway outside the church sanctuary so we could keep talking without the worry of keeping our voices down. Sometimes we needed to cry. Sometimes we needed to high-five each other and hug and freak out when someone got that new house or hit that weight goal or got approved for foster care. And all because I stopped using a Bible study as a footrest and decided to ask just one person if they'd be interested in getting together.

Then came the move to Maryland. And I was nervous, but I was also a whole lot more experienced at this "new girl" friend thing.

So once we'd moved into our new house. Once we'd finally found a church and started to navigate the new meet and greet, there was an announcement about new home groups. I looked over at Peter and he looked at me, and we knew we'd sign up because the meet and greet is never enough time and we're the newbies again. We also knew that in order to actually know the people around us, we needed to go get introduced. It helped that the young leader describing the new home group launch was so delighted at the idea herself you could almost feel the excitement radiating from her red hair and off her tiny frame.

I beelined it to her after the service and told her our story. We're new. We don't know anyone. But we have a house and a big yard, and we feel pretty sure God gave them to us so that we could fill them up with people. And just like that I was signing up to find out more about hosting a home group, then attending an informational meeting the next Saturday morning where I sat at the table with a bunch of strangers and shared my story. Again.

That's what it takes. Being willing to do the hard work of being awkwardly vulnerable with people you don't know yet but really hope to know. Being willing to trust that there's a Lisa or a Bobbi in the group clustered around a dining room table eating scrambled egg casserole and fruit salad at 11:00 a.m. in a neighborhood you still have to use MapQuest to navigate.

Newness takes time to wear off. It takes shared meals and text messages and laughter because you forgot a name you really, really should know by now, *again*. It takes willingness to walk down the block to the neighborhood cookout, or bring a dish to the church potluck, or show up for the gingerbread house-making afternoon with your kids. Being new takes time. Literally. And it's easy to become impatient and frustrated. Even my seven-year-old could tell you all about the excruciating pain of sending notes home with a friend, trying so desperately to schedule a play date, and then hearing nothing but silence in return. But my seven-year-old is teaching me persistence.

Because every afternoon for weeks after he climbed down off the school bus in our new neighborhood he would ask me, "Did they call, Mom?" And every afternoon I'd have to dread saying, "No." But he just kept asking. He just kept prodding. So I tried all different kinds of ways to get in touch with the parents of the new friend he was determined to make. We sent written notes with our contact info, and we asked his teacher to pass a note along until finally we had an e-mail address we could write to directly. We put ourselves out there. We admitted our newnes, and we vulnerably asked for that play date.

So the silence that came back and that stretched out for weeks wrapped itself around my chest and whispered, "It's not worth it." But I have a seven-year-old who never gave up. And the day we got an e-mail back, the day we got an explanation about crossed wires, was the day I told my son with totally legitimate tears in my eyes that his new friend was dying for him to come over for a play date on the spot. On the spot, man! Once we figured out how to get in touch and once they realized we hadn't received their initial reply, once we all moved past our awkward beginning, we landed in this sweet, sweet spot of a brand-new friendship right down the road. Because my kid wouldn't quit talking me out of my own insecurity as the new mom. Because my kid kept believing the best of his friend and their family. Because my kid was determined, *determined*, to connect, he never stopped hoping. Never stopped persevering. Never stopped believing. Not once.

So come January, we'll start hosting a home group in our house even though we're the newbies and my laziness is constantly in a headlock with my deep desire for friendship. But my hunger for connection knows that showing up is the only way to finding my way into community, into those late nights where it's safe to cry and freak out and laugh and snort all within the same ten minutes. I want that. I want that when I'm the new girl, and I want that for the new girls I meet.

So I'm going all in. I'm going to keep showing up and going first and telling my embarrassing stories because I've learned that it's when we let people see the un-Photoshopped parts of our lives that they're the most comfortable. I want people to see my dust bunnies and my doubts, my broken washing machine and my pretty new countertops, my most recent battle with lice in all three of my kids' hair as well as my delight in Christmas and the perfect spot we just found for our tree. All of it. I have to be willing to share all of it if I want to begin the process of chipping away at the pretend surfaces of being new and find ways to let people into all the places where I am the most real.

PART 2

WHAT *CAN'T* WE DO ABOUT IT?

In the beginning God made us in His image. It's the only image we're supposed to fit. The only image that won't make us feel like we can't breathe because everything is too tight or too uncomfortable or too itchy and scratchy in all the wrong places. We may try to cram ourselves, like the feet of Cinderella's sisters, into shoes that we were never meant to wear, but we won't be able to actually get anywhere in them. Those shoes, like those images in the latest magazine, Instagram feeds of houses you wish you owned, or Facebook updates of lives you wish you lived will always fit like that pair of jeans that cuts off your circulation and makes you hate all the parts of yourself that you can't shove into them. And, we're not supposed to hate ourselves. So you gotta think that images that make us hate ourselves don't fit because they aren't supposed to fit, right?

> *In the beginning God made us in His image. It's the only image we're supposed to fit.*

As uncomfortable as we feel when trying to stuff ourselves into those ridiculous images that were never designed with us in mind, we often, unintentionally, try and do the same to the people around us. In our relationships, maybe without even realizing it, we try to stuff our people into an image we've created for them. An image that's comfortable for us, but might actually cut off their circulation, their personality, their quirks. I've done this for years, often with the best intentions. I love people. I love seeing them grow into the best versions of themselves. The only problem is that it's not actually up to me to come up with the blueprint for that version. I'm not their God. And they're not supposed to be created in my image. You'd think I would have learned this earlier than year seventeen of marriage.

But I didn't. It's been a slow lesson. And it hasn't been until recently, more recent than you would likely believe, that it started to sink in. I was sitting in a hotel room late one night with smudgy mascara eyes and a book tucked up on the pillow in front of me when this quote by Frederick Buechner unfurled itself across my eyes and covered my whole body with goose bumps:

> Stop trying to protect, to rescue, to judge, to manage the lives around you . . . Remember that the lives of others are not your business. They are God's business. Even your own life is not your business. It is also God's business.[1]

I read that quote like I was hearing a voice in my head. Telling me to unclench my stubborn fists and let the people in my life breathe without judging them for how loud or how often or how annoying their breathing or eating or personalities or planning or habits sometimes are to me.

This is hard. This is hard because the mother in me is used to mothering the people around me. It started early when I mothered my poor younger brothers half around the bend with irritation in the wake of our mom dying. Because it's one thing to love the people around us; it's another to use that love like a tool to manipulate a certain outcome from them.

Love is that thing we're
supposed to give away
without any strings attached.

Love is that thing we're supposed to give away without any strings attached. But I'm learning about myself that often my love is really just a polite way of inviting someone else to do, act, or give me what I want, need, or have to have in order to feel good about myself. This is as unhealthy as trying to fit myself back into the "juniors section" jeans I used to be able to wear three babies and one decade ago.

That's what this section is about. It's an honest look at whether we're trying to create friendships in our image or whether we're honestly accepting them on their own terms. Because the thing is, being human by definition means we're surrounded by other humans. And because we're not simply clones, we're going to get offended, frustrated, and wish we could change the way other people do friendship. Growth is one thing. Growth is healthy. Growth is good.

> **People come in all shapes and sizes and stories and it's not our job to fix them, use them, or get them to act just like us. It's our job to love them.**

But manipulation and control are completely different. They try to rewrite the stories of the people around us into a version that suits us better. That's more convenient for us. That makes them in our own image. And often we do it out of our own fear. Out of our own past hurts. Out of the desperate desire to control our interactions with other people. That instinct has been around for a long time. The instinct not to trust the people around us. The author of Psalm 118 wrote about it thousands of years ago: "It is better to take refuge in the LORD than to trust in man" (v. 8).

We want control because we've been wounded by trust. We like manipulation because it looks a lot like love, and it comes with the guarantee that we get what we want out of a relationship.

This section of the book is about letting go of that compulsion. Letting go of the belief that we can control other people's stories or expect other people to fill up all our empty, lonely places or that we can always have friendship our way and on our terms. If you've been alive long enough to read these words, you've lived long enough to know that's simply not possible. Trying to force friendships into our image usually involves much more grief than letting God remake us in His own image with access to His own bottomless resources of love.

People come in all shapes and sizes and stories, and it's not our job to fix them, use them, or get them to act just like us. It's our job to love them. In fact, it's our job to go to the very outer limits of our capabilities when we hear the word *love*. It's more than a feeling. It's the commitment to care about someone more than yourself, and then to take action steps to ensure that other person's well-being—their "shalom."[2]

The Bible is super frank on this point—along with how hard it can sometimes be—so I'm pretty sure none of us are going to get it all right all the time. The point is the trying, isn't it? And ultimately, it's a relief when we wake up to the fact that we're not supposed to be the architect of the people around us. Because who can live up to that kind of pressure? Who wants to? It's exhausting to constantly try to change people and remake them in our own image. It's disappointing to constantly wait for them to do or choose friendship like we do or choose friendship.

Because, as Beth Moore writes, "Even if we are unselfish and undistracted enough to give another person our all for an indefinite period of time, can we save them from themselves? I don't think so."[3] That job belongs to their Maker, the master Creator who breathed their blueprint into life and who gave Himself up to death in order to put them back together in His own image.

So here's to the things about friendship that we can't fix, and that aren't even our job to fix. Here's to the things that aren't ours to control—here's to the permission to stop trying. May we figure out the difference before it's too late, and before we've worried and nagged and micromanaged our friendships to death.

Here's to the freedom to let people be themselves—in all their glorious ranges of shapes and sizes and maturity, hair color, work preferences, passions, communication styles, and stories. Here's to not trying to fit our friendships into a pair of jeans that we couldn't possibly sit down in. Here's to friendships that leave room to breathe.

WE CAN'T ALWAYS HAVE FRIENDSHIP OUR WAY

"There have been several people in my life, who I never would've picked as friends because they were SO different from me, but I see God's leading in bringing them into my life to challenge me to see and love as He does and to challenge and inspire me to grow." —Anna[1]

FEMALE FRIENDSHIP SEEMS TO come complete with a secret guide-book, handshake, and hair style—often dependent on your little part of the world—that can leave every single woman at some point or another standing on the sidelines, unsure what to do, say, or initiate to help her navigate her way inside the clubhouse.

And while there's a constant see-saw of who's up and who's down when it comes to making the rules, each of us knows what it's like to walk straight into a wall of expectation you didn't even realize existed. Because control makes us feel safe, we start to practice it in elementary school—where we can be quick to point out to the girls at our table what they did wrong and what disqualifies them from being our friend.

Junior high girls vote each other out of their friendship circles. But grown-up women do it too. With more subtlety and no less cruelty.

But friendship can't survive in an atmosphere of control. We can't connect when we're setting all the terms. So it's essential we identify the often unrealistic expectations we bring into friendships—and how those can disappoint us before we've even begun. And I hope this conversation serves as a signpost pointing back to the example of Jesus who gave up heaven and earth, platform and title, to move into the neighborhood and live alongside the people He wanted to befriend. He came to be the friend—to connect with us in our language, on our terms, and right alongside our messes.

It Would Be So Much Easier If No One Disagreed with Me

There's a toddler living inside of me who wants to get her own way all the time, all the ways she possibly could, all the livelong day. And if I'm being as brutally honest as toddlers tend to be at the most inconvenient times, I'd admit that life would be so much easier if people always saw my side, always shared my opinions, always got where I was coming from. Life would be so much less complicated if no one questioned what I thought or told me they thought something different.

If only I never felt misunderstood or rubbed the wrong way. If I felt confident and right all the time, maybe I would sleep more. Community can be so uncomfortable. It can chafe and irritate and misunderstand even our best intentions.

It will irk you and stretch you, and some days you will be tempted to run and hide and whisper to yourself, "I'd be a great Christian if it weren't for other people always messing it up." Yup, I've thought that. Gross, right? But sadly, it's true. Admitting that out loud is probably the first step toward getting out of my own way when it comes to connecting with people instead of trying to control them. In their book *Safe People: How to Find Relationships That Are Good for You and Avoid Those That Aren't*, Drs. Cloud and Townsend remind us that, "We first have to face the ways that we are part of the problem before we can become a redemptive agent in the life of someone else."[2] So this is me, facing it.

And the only way I've really had any success when it comes to derailing those gross thoughts is by admitting that I can't actually stuff someone else's feelings or opinions into a response that suits me, that fits me, or that is all about making me feel good. Nope. Interacting with people solely on your own terms or your own agenda or your own time line or preference for communication is manipulation, no matter how we dress it up.

Instead, I'm learning that really loving people means loving them the way they need to be loved, not the way you like being loved. Drs. Cloud and Townsend describe it like this,

> We need to give up our expectations for people to be faultless or to be basically different from who they really are. Maybe the person isn't so "bad" after all; maybe they are just different than we would have made them. Maybe what we are thinking is the absolute "right" way to be or to live is really a personal preference that we are trying to legislate on someone else. We tend to make our view the "right" view, even in areas where God says that other views are okay also. This is the whole concept of Christian freedom.[3]

It might surprise you to know how old I finally was before this lesson fully sank in. I remember standing in the tiny shower of our rental house a couple years ago crying mad, frustrated tears while staring at the white tiles, because someone I loved, someone close to me, was shutting me out of a part of their life.

I remember wondering how someone so close to me could be so deeply resistant to talking through a similar painful history. Or be so stubbornly angry anytime I tried to peel back the past so that we could make sense of this shared future we were supposed to have inherited together.

Over and over again throughout the day I'd ask my husband the age-old question of every child, "But *why*? Why can't I tell her I need to process this with her?" And Peter would go back to the beginning and explain it as if to a very young child, "Because she's already processed that pain. You want her to go back again and process it with you. That will make you feel better, but not her."

And then the kicker: "Doing that doesn't make her feel loved. It only makes you feel loved. If you really want to love her the way you say you do, you'll respect that and love her on her own terms."

So I'd stand in the shower and cry instead of e-mail, text, or call because my nature feels loved the most through words. I wanted to pour out all my words and all my questions and talk in circles right around and over and through the hard and painful things I recently discovered had happened to her. Instead, I stood in the shower and cried. It was so hard to bite my tongue and simply listen. It was so hard to show up on her terms instead of my own. It was so hard not to insist that she let me talk out all my feelings that had sprung up like loud, shouty, little monsters all demanding attention ever since we'd sat across from each other over burgers and fries, and I'd realized how badly I'd missed so many details of her life.

All I wanted to do was talk and make it better, and all she wanted to do was share the facts and then move forward.

I was angry that I didn't get to have my say. She was angry that I thought I had a say in something that had happened to her. Everything was complicated by the long distance between us. And so I went to Peter to tell him how hurt I was and how I couldn't understand why she wouldn't process with me, "Like any other normal person."

To which he smiled and reminded me that I'm not, in fact, the definition of normal. What works for me doesn't work for everyone else. And if I wanted real relationship again with her, it would have to be on her terms. If I was serious about loving this friend who was like a little sister, I would have to love her in a way that she could understand. I'd have to speak the kind of love that was her native language. Turns out, we don't all speak the same love languages. And it's hard to lisp your way through someone else's native love tongue.

When we're at that kind of standoff, I see three choices: (1) you can demand they see things your way; (2) you can write them off; (3) or you can get over yourself and decide to see the world through their eyes, love them through their heart, support them through their passions.

It took me a solid nine months.

Nine months of frustration. Nine months of biting my tongue and focusing on where she was at, what she was up to, what made her feel supported rather than what would have made me feel understood. I took steps into her world and made myself focus on her more than on me. It's humbling to admit how hard that was. And that over two years later it still doesn't come naturally to me. Our own heads are so filled up with our own point of view that it is very, very hard to get out of our own way to make room for someone else. We are so predisposed to what suits us, what's convenient for us, what feels good to us, that it's like signing up for some kind of friendship boot camp when we make the decision to relentlessly love someone in a way that's more about them than it is about us.

In the words of Bob Goff, "If we make loving people a strategy for something else, it isn't love."[4] And as I wrestled through wanting resolution my own way versus offering understanding in a way that was foreign to me, I kept thinking about Jesus. It's so humbling how He came to us. How He literally didn't "consider equality with God as something to be used for His own advantage. Instead, He emptied Himself by assuming the form of a slave, taking on the likeness of men" (Phil. 2:6b–7a). And as if that wasn't enough He went on, relentlessly, humbly meeting us at the very crossroads of our own inability to change from our sinful ways and His reckless generosity to accomplish even that on our own behalf.

Have you ever really just sat with those words and imagined them? Really thought them through—how the God who constructed the universe and the sun and the moon as they hung in the skies over Bethlehem, the God who knew how many breaths per minute Mary took and how many hairs were on her head, came and folded Himself up into her DNA nestled right under her heartbeat, beneath her lungs.

How the God who put the earth on its axis and then flung the infinite burning stars into being and the solar system into orbit, reduced Himself to finite time and space and knelt down in front of the men who didn't really understand Him and washed each of their sweaty, muddy feet (John 13:1–20). How He inconvenienced Himself for thirty-three years until He was murdered on false charges by people who arrested Him under false pretenses.

He didn't take advantage of a single one of heaven's home-court advantages.

He just kept on letting Himself be inconvenienced until He literally couldn't take another step or another breath.

But when we ignore His example, when we're so invested in getting our own way, then we're not being friends, we're being polite, masterful manipulators. Manipulation equals, "I want you to act a certain way so that I can feel a certain way." But love, love equals, "I want the best for you no matter how it makes me feel."

And it can make me feel not-good. Friendship that makes me care more about my friend than myself can annoy and leave me looking for a quick exit or an excuse not to have to deal. We're so used to putting ourselves first, living for our own convenience and comfort. Just consider every late-night infomercial designed to underline the message that everything around us should cater to making our lives easier for just $19.99 and free shipping. It can be a radically uncomfortable exercise to give up the right to have friendship just the way we've always liked it.

We Are Called to More Than Unfriending Each Other

We have so many friendship channels at our disposal these days, what with Facebook and Instagram and Twitter and Snapchat and I could go on and on but I'm sure I'm too old to be in the know about every kind of social media that's currently blowing up phones around the world.

Each has its own niche in the online world, but they've all taught us that friends can be "liked" or "un-liked" and "unfriended" with the swipe of one finger. I wonder if we've forgotten there are people behind those pixels. That God "uses people to change people."[5] That it's the inconvenient and the uncomfortable friendships God can most effectively use to teach us His fruits of the Spirit—how to put into practice "love, joy, peace, patience, kindness, goodness, faith, gentleness, [and] self-control" (Gal. 5:22–23) in real time alongside real people who push all of our very real buttons.

Changing the channel on friendships the way we would on the radio or with the swipe of a Facebook selection isn't recommended if we actually want to know and be known by the people God has trusted us to love on His behalf. My friend Holley compares it to our instinct to punch the radio dial and change the channel anytime the music starts to annoy us or isn't to our taste. "My approach of instantly switching the station when I get into my husband's vehicle isn't recommended for relationships. We can deal with those who are different than us by immediately trying to make them change to be like us.

But doing so is not only dishonoring (perhaps even offensive), it also keeps us from learning and growing."[6]

Changing the channel on friendship is a lot messier than it is on a radio station. If we simply disconnect, cut off, or walk out on anyone who is no longer a good "friendship fit" or doesn't suit our "friendship taste," then before long we're going to leave a lot of hurt and confused people in our wake.

True friendship, real friendship, velveteen friendship will chip away parts of ourselves that we'd grown fond of. It will chafe against our quirks and question our beliefs. It will wriggle down into our doubts and bring them to light.

Friendship will mold us, and we will feel it. Because we're supposed to: "As iron sharpens iron, so a friend sharpens a friend" (Prov. 27:17 NLT). The minute we open our doors, our laptops, our comment boxes, our homes, our churches, our celebrations to others, we simultaneously open our hearts. People will come in and traipse great, big, muddy, footprints all over the spaces and places we hold sacred. "We don't learn to love each other well in the easy moments. Anyone is good company at a cocktail party. But love is born when we misunderstand one another and make it right. When we cry in the kitchen, when we show up uninvited with magazines and granola bars, in an effort to say, I love you."[7]

And if we want real friendship that goes beyond politeness or car pool or small talk, we must sacrifice. We must sacrifice the pretty perceptions we've built of others and ourselves. We must sacrifice our pedestals, our distance, and our time. We must sacrifice our long lists of wants, demands, and expectations. We must lay them down and be willing to have them completely upended. Crumpled. Rearranged. Messed up.

If it is real, friendship is usually untidy. If it is lasting, friendship will hit road bumps and potholes, and we'll get shaken up and sometimes bruised along the way. And then when it becomes more than just a polite exchange of "I'm fine thanks, how're you?" friendship starts to get that lived-in look. Crumbs and stray socks and leftovers you forgot to put back into the fridge. And sometimes it feels awkward until one afternoon you find that the messy is starting to blend into the comfortable. And in the midst of sacrificing what we wanted out of friendship, we discover what God was planning for us all along.

This unwrapped beauty. This ordinary wonder. This pretzel of imperfect. This sweet understanding. If we can just get brave enough, countercultural enough, to eradicate the thought that unfriending people who don't suit us is our right, and instead remember that our role model—Jesus—sank His entire self into just twelve friends. A small circle. A circle that included hotheads and doubters and friends who would fall asleep when He needed them most. Friends who swore they'd never known Him and sold out His friendship to people who wanted to kill Him. Twelve men who were horribly imperfect, constantly misunderstood Him, and were often inconvenient to Him in the worst ways.

> *If we can just get brave enough,*
> *countercultural enough, to eradicate*
> *the thought that unfriending people*
> *who don't suit us is our right.*

But Jesus didn't leave, unlike, or unfriend a single one of them. Not even when they deserved it. Not even when they swore they'd never met Him, didn't know Him, despised what He stood for. Instead, He kept on keeping His promise, first made through Moses in Genesis, that He would never leave or forsake His people (Deut. 31:6). Jesus kept on being a friend right up to, through, and across the bitter finish line and then continued to pursue them across the span of His own death and life again. In His final prayer, His heart-felt correspondence with His Father God on the night before He would die, He testified to His own faithfulness as a friend to the twelve men He'd called by name: "While I was with them, I was protecting them by Your name that You have given Me. I guarded them and not one of them is lost, except the son of destruction, so that the Scripture may be fulfilled" (John 17:12).

Facebook might try to teach us that friendship is defined by how wide and far and massive our reach, our circles, and our name. But if we will only let Jesus' example remind us that the kind of friend we are will always be measured by depth, by commitment, by being determined to keep trying over and over again.

Jesus could tell His Father, in no uncertain terms, that as far as it was possible for Him, He had kept the faith and the friendship of every one of the men entrusted to Him. Even Judas had been included right up until the moment he chose to quit Jesus, not the other way around.

Don't quit your friendships because they're uncomfortable. Don't quit your friendships to avoid conflict. Don't unfriend your friends because they're annoying or because they haven't lived up to your expectations. Instead, ask yourself what you can do to "guard" them as Jesus guarded His friends—this Greek word He used meant the kind of protection you'd get "behind the walls of a fortress."[8]

How can we be safe spaces for our friends instead of trying to make them, manipulate them, or unfriend them to force them into conforming to our own images? Instead of building walls *between* us when they don't react in a way that meets our expectations, how can we build a wall of trust, of guilt-free friendship, *around* them so that they can let their guard down with us? How can we become willing to be inconvenienced by friendship?

For me it was beginning with the simple realization that should probably have dawned on me decades ago—friendship will, indeed, inconvenience you. More so if you're doing it right. If you've never been annoyed, put out, or interrupted by a friendship, then you're likely holding out and missing out. Because in the words of one of my favorite storybook characters, the Skin Horse from *The Velveteen Rabbit*, friendships, like people, become their most real when we aren't afraid of having our rough edges loved off. And it doesn't happen all at once or just with one person. And it will sometimes hurt.[9]

Friendship will, indeed, inconvenience you. More so if you're doing it right. If you've never been annoyed, put out, or interrupted by a friendship, then you're likely holding out and missing out.

Becoming real in our friendships means we'll let our friends love off our expectations and we'll let go of trying to change them and instead begin to enjoy them. Like that pair of Sunday-afternoon jeans. The ones that sag a bit in the knees because they're so worn in. The ones that are more comfortable because of all the knocks and stretches and washes they've been through. The ones that don't fit perfectly when measured by fashion's standards. The ones that fit perfectly because they're perfectly worn in and you feel the most like yourself—your ordinary, everyday self—when you're wearing them.

WE CAN'T EXPECT OTHER PEOPLE TO FILL US UP

*"It's an effort not to find my identity in being liked and accepted
by others but rather in being loved and forgiven by Christ."*
—Heidi[1]

SOME DAYS—GOODNESS, some *years*—we are running on empty. We
are weary and wrung out and bone dry and desperate for a cool, fresh glass
of encouragement or appreciation or for someone to just simply see us. And
it's wonderful when we get that encouragement from our friends. That is an
element of friendship, yes.

However, if we are constantly disappointed by how our friends don't live
up to our need for encouragement, the problem might be that we're expecting the kind of soul validation they're not equipped to give. The kind of soul
validation that one person who may have had a bad Monday and already feels
stressed by her kids or her looming work deadline can't possibly provide. No,
that greedy, desperate black hole hungry for affirmation, acceptance, love, and
validation down in our guts will never be satisfied by what humans dole out
in small, limited portions of approval. That universe-sized hole needs a universe-sized being to fill it up. It needs a God.

Latching on to a friend with the hope that they will give us God-sized affirmation will always disappoint. This is neither our friend's fault nor our own.
This is simply how we're designed. The user manual for humanity spells out specifically that God and only God can give us the words and the lives that fill us up,

You make known to me the path of life;
in your presence there is fullness of joy;
at your right hand are pleasures forevermore. (Ps. 16:11 ESV)

Our friends can never promise that. They aren't equipped to give us "pleasures forevermore," no matter how kind or generous they might be. They're simply not equipped to be the sole source of our personal contentment. And if we expect them to be, we should expect a whole hurt of dissatisfaction and misunderstanding.

By the same token, there will also be people in our lives who are like the old metaphor of the bucket with a hole in the bottom—no matter how much we pour into them, it will never be enough to fill them (or their confidence, self-image, or need for approval) up.

Both dynamics will sap a friendship. Both need balance. But both are the result of being designed for unadulterated God-approval. Apologist and pastor in New York City, witness to fame seekers and hungry unbelievers, Tim Keller writes in *The Freedom of Self-Forgetfulness*, "What Paul is looking for, what Madonna is looking for, what we are all looking for, is an ultimate verdict that we are important and valuable."[2] Ain't that the truth. Problem is, we'll never get it to our satisfaction from other people.

Other People Can't Satisfy Your Soul Cravings

The prophet Jeremiah wrote, "Your words were found, and I ate them. Your words became a delight to me and the joy of my heart" (Jer. 15:16). I don't know about you, but I have a ravenous appetite for the words of other people. The words of affirmation, the words of invitation and compliment and confirmation. My appetite for that kind of approval seems like some kind of bottomless hole. If left to its own natural inclinations, my delight in pleasing people and gobbling up their pleasing affirmation would gorge itself till it was sick with the approval of others. And still it would never be satisfied. Because you can't live on that kind of approval. That kind of approval is temporary, insubstantial, and just when you think you need it most, it will likely disappear like that bag of cotton candy that evaporated into nothing but sticky, dried-up sugar overnight.

The words Jeremiah is talking about—God's words—are meat-and-potatoes type of words. Words with substance. Words made to last, to fill, to comfort like hot stew on a cold winter night. Words from the God who has always used His words to fill up nothingness. In the beginning, when there was only vast emptiness, God spoke light and day and night and creeping, crawling, swimming, flying animals and growing, spreading, twining plants and trees and unfathomably deep oceans into existence. God's words build something out of nothing. God's words have substance to them.

You can bite into God's words and chew them and be nourished like so much bread baked fresh and lathered in butter and eaten while still steaming hot. Surely these must be the kind of words Jesus had in mind when He deflected Satan's temptation to turn stones into bread for His starving stomach by saying, "Man must not live on bread alone but on every word that comes from the mouth of God" (Matt. 4:4). God's words are more satisfying than even the freshest, warmest, most tempting baked loaves of French bread.

But I forget. I have a kind of God-amnesia that haunts me because I'm constantly drawn back to other people for sustenance. It's an instinct I have to fight. And usually I only remember when I get to the end of a day and find myself hungrier and crabbier than when the day started. After I've spent hours mindlessly surfing the Internet for something to fill me up, I always, *always*, look up feeling gross and empty. But it's where I tend to go when I'm feeling restless and unsettled in my skin and I want instant gratification. If God's words are hearty, loaded mashed potatoes, then looking for affirmation online tastes like the powdered, instant, just-add-water, soupy version of those same mashed potatoes. But it's where I go when I need a quick fix, when I'm putting off doing the things I should be doing. When I feel anxious and needy, I mindlessly scroll the Internet looking for something to fill me up and get rid of that shaky feeling. I'm like a junkie looking for an approval fix.

I can spend hours clicking from one link to another, from one viral video to the next news analysis, from that current trending meme to the blog of the person I wish I could write like. But all I feel by the end of that kind of mindless consumption is a stomachache. Or maybe it's more of a soul ache.

I feel lonelier and emptier than I did when I opened the first browser.

My husband teases me that of the five love languages, my top ones are "all of them." And it's true. I love gifts and acts of service and touch and quality time together. But I really, really love words. I love hearing someone tell me I did a good job on something. I love someone taking the time to drop me a note or an e-mail or a voice message just to share something they noticed I did well. I even love hearing from my kids how much those piles of clean laundry mean to them. Maybe it's more accurate to say I *especially* love hearing from my people when I've sweated and wrestled over dinner or laundry or cleaning their apocalyptic rooms.

Words of affirmation are so motivating to me that I've been known to prompt my husband when to say them and exactly what to say. Seventeen years into marriage and I've finally figured out that he isn't a mind reader. We finally stopped having fights about things he didn't say or do when I realized that I couldn't expect him to intuit my every need and emotion. That life is, in fact, not like my favorite romantic comedies, and that the guy needs an assist if he's going to say the right thing at the right time.

For example, a couple weeks back Pete and the kids had been out for a few hours and instead of fitting in some quality binge reading, I wrestled the sink full of dishes into submission, swept, vacuumed, and mopped our home back into livable standards. I was so proud of my achievement and knew from years of mismanaged expectations that if my family didn't fall over themselves in gasps of reverent awe at what I'd accomplished, I'd be fuming and they'd be completely befuddled by my behavior.

So I did what any woman who's finally learned from having the exact same fight hundreds of times does—I called Peter and told him exactly what I'd done and exactly how I'd like him and the kids to respond when they walked in the door. You might think this is Looney Tunes kind of behavior. But I know myself and my family well enough to know that communication about expectations gives us all a head start on having an evening together that doesn't end in temper tantrums (often my own).

And they went above and beyond. That kooky, awesome family walked in the door, and perfectly coached by Peter, all three kids immediately began oohing and ahhing over the state of the house. They walked around the kitchen like it was something straight out of a Disney movie come to life—such were their levels of ecstasy and awe. They applauded. They cheered and clapped and hugged me, and it didn't last more than five minutes, but during that time I felt so profoundly loved and filled up that the fact that I'd prompted the entire exchange was entirely beside the point.

Peter knows my primary love language, and he's a hoot when he leads the kids in all kinds of whooping and hollering cheers of appreciation over a clean kitchen. But my craving for approval in words and preferably long sentences filled with adjectives can be a sneaky thing. It can grow uber loud and demanding, and it can forget that kind words from others are a gift and not supposed to be a hostage situation—your kind words in exchange for my kind attitude.

There have been nights that stand out vividly in my memory from our early years of marriage. Nights when Peter and I fought each other in relentless circles, him patiently trying to meet my needs for processing or approval or conversation or emoting until he's run flat out of words and I'm still not satisfied. And on one of those nights, I was stunned to hear my young husband point out to me that, "I just can't be all things to you. I can't be the perfect husband and the perfect girlfriend and the perfect answer to all your questions. You need other people besides just me."

As a newlywed it was disappointing to me. Disappointing to discover that my husband wouldn't be the answer to all my needs for emotional and spiritual input. But I've lived a lot more years of marriage since then. And looking back I know that was one of the most profound things Peter has ever taught me. That one person can't possibly be the source of all the needs and wants and demands and hopes and expectations for another person. I've learned that in my marriage. And I'm finally learning it in my friendships too.

But it's taken awhile. It's taken a long and sometimes unhealthy while to unwrap myself from constantly needing a top up from a friendship to feel necessary and valued. One of my top five themes on the Strengths Finders profile is Empathy. Being able to feel what other people around me are feeling is my superpower. It's also my kryptonite. If I feel a tremor under the surface of a friendship, I feel equally compelled to understand it and fix it. Which often leaves me hostage to the feelings of others. Sometimes, friendships are on their own timetable and we can't fast-forward them to a place where everything is copacetic. Which, in turn, leaves me in long, awful, unvalidated stretches where a friend is no longer giving me even subtle pats on the head of friendship approval. Instead, the friendship has hit a speed bump, and I can hear the gears grinding as we try to find our way over it. In the meantime, all my empathy sensors are blaring and my approval tank is empty and it can make me do crazy things.

It can make me try to invent ways to get that friend to connect, to circle back around and open her heart to me again, to say out loud what I'm craving to hear in my shameless spiral of neediness—that I'm funny or kind or that she loved that book I recommended. Most of the time what's happening with that friend isn't even about me. But my "I need affirmation or I might die" tank is relentless. And only by gritting my teeth and literally ignoring it and that pit in my stomach can I get myself to remember that no matter what they say or don't say, no one person should be able to hold that kind of power over my emotional well-being.

I am learning to tame the greedy need for other people to fill me up. Or using them for my own emotional satisfaction—most of the time without even realizing that was my true motivation. Because I think this perversion of friendship is absolutely one of Satan's disgusting end games—to see you and me behave like some kind of emotional leeches, sucking all the approval and validation out of the people around us, so that we can feel whole again. To turn our friends into our sustenance.

Doing so flips friends into our idols as well as our masters. We are at their beck and emotional call while simultaneously curating our own behavior so that it flatters, manipulates, and squeezes out a reaction that satisfies our insatiable souls.

In Exodus 20, God clearly states in His Ten Commandments to the people of Israel, "You shall have no other gods before me" (v. 3 NIV). When we are unable to function without the approval of certain people, we have made them our gods. We have raised them up to positions of control in our lives they were never intended to occupy. Nothing will rot a healthy relationship faster than this kind of abdication. "If we need any one person in order to survive, we will not be able to resolve the relationship."[3]

We can't keep giving those craven instincts a pass. We need to start paying attention. When the urge for validation from another person rises up in us we need to recognize it for what it is—a signpost. I'm starting to do that. Finally. To learn to spot those panicked urges for approval as a big, loud, screaming neon sign that my universe-sized hunger for affirmation needs to go running to the universe-sized God. Not that I should start mindlessly scrolling Facebook, or checking to see how many likes my last Instagram post got, but that I should literally recognize my approval panic attacks as they're happening.

For me, this looks like pushing pause in the moment. Whatever that moment happens to look like. Sometimes it means closing my laptop. Sometimes it means putting my phone in a different room. And instead, getting my hands into the things that ground me. The things that can't be manipulated or pleased. The things that are true, regardless of me or my outcomes.

That can be as simple as straightening up leftover art projects and daily mess. It can look like walking outside my back door and staring into the woods. Sometimes it's taking out the trash and jumping up and down on the boxes that need to be flattened before they can be recycled. Maybe it's opening an old book that reads like a trusted, unchanging friend. The things that remind me of my place in the world. They don't need to look deeply spiritual from the outside. But I'm convinced that by filling my mind with the things that are "true, noble, reputable, authentic, compelling, gracious—the best, not the worst; the beautiful, not the ugly; things to praise, not things to curse" (Phil. 4:8–9 MSG), I will turn my attention back to the God who makes all those things possible. The God who isn't just a king of wishful thinking but a guarantor of promises that I will find my worth, my calling, and my ultimate purpose and approval in Him.

It's such an insane relief. To put down my phone. To stop trolling the Internet. To stop waiting for her reply to my e-mail, my phone call, my tentative, humiliating need for validation. To, instead, let myself fall deeply, fully, wholly into the great, insanely unlimited, bottomless tank of God's approval. To bite into and chew on the truth that He delights in me and sings over me (Zeph. 3:17 NIV). That He literally will leave a roomful of other people to come chasing after me (Matt. 18:12) on the days I'm feeling lost and angsty for approval. That He is never tired of me always needing Him. That instead, He is delighted by how desperately I need His validation and He never, ever withholds it from me. Or from you.

> *Jesus is never tired of me always needing Him. Instead, He is delighted by how desperately I need His validation and He never, ever withholds it from me. Or from you.*

That He calls us beloved and beautiful. That I am His and He is mine and I can hang on every word that comes out of His mouth (Matt. 4:4) and that there will always be more than enough words to fill me up because He is generous and happily lists out the hundreds of ways He loves me with the same extravagant attention to detail as He spends knowing how many hairs are on my insecure head (Luke 12:7). And that kind of security? It can change a girl. It tattoos acceptance into her bones. And teaches her to let go of her death grip on the opinions of others. It's a feast. A meat and potatoes and triple-layer chocolate cake for dessert feast. So that even on the days when the doubts circle overhead and twinges of hunger for someone else's approval threaten, then even the leftovers of a God-sized meal like that are enough to fill me up and keep the rest at bay.

I Believe in Guilt-Free Friendship

When you live in between countries like I do, then friendship takes extra intentional work. You'll know what I mean if you live far from your parents or family or if you've moved recently and are still trying to keep in touch with all your old circles of friends, even if it's just to a new neighborhood in your old town or graduating from college. It's hard. Relationships take work, and they'll slowly die off like most of the plants under my care if we don't tend to them and water them with regular time, conversations, and interest.

The real test comes when a whole lot of time has ticked by, and it's been ages since we talked or e-mailed or whatever form of communication is your jam. Sometimes it just feels awkward trying to reconnect. Especially if you suspect that your friend might be annoyed that she's sent the last three e-mails and you're now in her e-mail debt. I often go e-mail bankrupt. Especially when it comes to friends who mean the most to me. Because I so badly want each note to be thoughtful and jam-packed with all the details we've missed in each other's lives. And when I can't construct that kind of note, I occasionally just give up altogether. Lame, I know.

It gets worse when you worry that all the time and letters that have gone by unreturned have built up a wall of friendship frustration. It's hard to catch up when there's first a big ol' ditch of guilt you have to hurdle over. So, my long-distance friends and I have started this thing we call "Guilt-Free Friendship."

Guilt-free friendship says that anytime you get back to me is a good time. Guilt-free friendship says that I will always assume the best about your motivations. Guilt-free friendship says that I won't keep score when it comes to e-mails answered or phone calls returned. Guilt-free friendship focuses on the friendship and ditches the guilt. Guilt-free friendship loves any chance and any slice of time to catch up; it isn't about criticizing how much or how frequently that happens. Instead, guilt-free friendship is generous and forgiving and creates easy space for reconnecting because it doesn't have any conditions for how or when or how often that happens.

Guilt-free friendship is the gift that women who are secure in their own sense of acceptance can give each other.

Guilt-free friendship is the gift that women who are secure in their own sense of acceptance can give each other. It's an impossible gift when we're taking our worth and measuring our validation by the frequency with which we hear from each other. Instead, anchoring our identity in the God who is obsessed with spending time with us makes us freely available to give grace to our friends who literally, humanly aren't able to make themselves that kind of available. When we are convinced that our lives bring delight to a God who views us with such an all-consuming passion that He would choose to woo us, love us, die for us, sing over us, and celebrate us, then we are women who can give each other the gift of guilt-free friendship.

This is the key to becoming women who don't depend on the schedules or generosity or the emotional roller coasters of others to fill us up. Take it from a woman who has cruised her Instagram comments from a bathroom stall because she was so anxious for acceptance. It will be the greatest relief of your life to stop waiting on someone else to give you permission to feel good about yourself. It will remake you and liberate you to believe that there's a God more passionate about you than the ending of any Jane Austen novel. So let Him. Just let Him.

WE CAN'T CONTROL OTHER PEOPLE'S STORIES

"Often we want to take control rather than allow God to move into spaces and others' hearts. Maybe we are trying to still control the outcome." —Chelsey[1]

YOU'VE HEARD IT SAID that broken people have sharp edges. This is that story. Because there are also lonely people, hurt people, and people with backgrounds so radically different from ours that, while we might both be speaking English, our friendship gets totally lost in translation because we don't have a common relationship language.

Whether we like it or not, we all haul some kind of baggage with us into our adult friendships. And we all need to be reminded that we're not responsible for the luggage that other women will bring with them. But that we will be impacted by it and should be ready for when those suitcases of junk inevitably explode at inconvenient times, when all you thought you were doing was making plans for a kids' play date and instead you end up down a dark and twisting conversation you never expected.

This is about taking Romans 12:18 (NIV) literally when it says, "If it is possible, as far as it depends on you, live at peace with everyone." We only know *if it is possible* if we have done all we can. Once we have, then we can know that we are the kind of people who are safe and inviting places for friendship, undaunted by the hard or heavy stories our friends bring with them into our friendships. It also means learning how to release ourselves from the false guilt we so often feel at the thought of walking away from an unhealthy friendship—one that as far as it is possible, *as far as it depends on you,* you haven't been able to fix. Giving ourselves permission to forgive the hurt of a friendship and still walk away from it is a necessary life skill. But emphasis on *the walk*. This isn't about running away from friends or quitting friendships or ruthlessly cutting inconvenient friends out of your life. This is about becoming safe people for the sake of ourselves and our friends.

It's Not Your Job to Rescue Other People. It's Your Job to Love Them.

One of my favorite cousins lives in South Africa. She has been like a surrogate mom to me over the years and her husband is a doctor. Several years ago he suffered an accidental needle prick. It comes with the territory in the medical field. But for a long, terrible while he didn't know if he had been infected with a virus or not.

It was a hard load to live under.

They didn't tell their kids the source of their worry. But children internalize their parents' anxiety. And their small frames and hearts got heavier and more stooped over under the weight of the worry they could feel in their house. They kept trying to carry it with their small hands and positive attitudes and big eyes, wanting to ask questions they were afraid to hear answers to. They could tell their parents were struggling with an unspoken fear, and the littles kept breathing in that air of anxiety until it became part of their own DNA, and they adopted that unspoken worry like it was their own. And of course, it almost crushed their tiny frames.

So my cousin and her husband intervened. One night after supper they lined up all three children (at the time aged six and under). A game of pretend was initiated, and each kid was given their school backpack to put on. And their parents followed them around the house and yard slowly, methodically adding rocks to the backpacks.

Big, hard, heavy stones. They kept filling the backpacks with those rocks.

At first the children enjoyed the challenge. They could do it. They could still run and play with the heavy packs. But rock after rock had them slowing down. Until all three were at a standstill and the game had lost its fun.

"We can't do this, Dad," said their oldest daughter.

"Why? Why can't you?" her father pushed back.

"Because they're too heavy. We're just kids; they're too heavy for us."

Tired, worried eyes looked out from scrunched-up faces at their parents. And the parents? They did what parents do.

They began unpacking their children's anxieties.

They acknowledged the ominous dread that had entered the house and that the kids had taken to carrying upon themselves. They slowly and clearly explained that this worry was not a weight designed for children. That it was too heavy for them. That managing it or carrying it or even trying to balance it was not up to them. They were not required to bear their parents' fears.

And with that, they reached into the backpacks that had been dragging down three sets of small shoulders and began to unpack them. They removed each of those heavy, hard rocks and hurled them into the back garden. The children got in on the spirit of the thing. Satchel straps slipped off small arms. Eager hands grabbed at ugly burdens and threw them far away.

Until those kids were free of the baggage that never belonged to them in the first place.

Sometimes friendship can feel like that. Sometimes, without even realizing we're doing it, we start accumulating the heavy rocks and sharp pieces of glass that our friends have been carrying and we put them into our own backpacks. We stuff ourselves full of our friends' hurts and frustrations and heavy, difficult stories, and then we wonder why it's so hard to keep walking forward.

Here's where it gets tricky. As Christians we're taught that it's a good thing to be willing to "bear one another's burdens" (Gal. 6:2 ESV). If we aren't careful, that can guilt us into putting up with a lot of behavior that is harmful to us. Being willing to "bear one another's burdens" is not the same as being willing to bear one another's dysfunction, rage, inappropriate behavior, manipulation, passive aggression, cruelty, control, and a whole host of other traits that we can inhale like secondhand smoke in some friendships without even being aware of it.

Even when we're neck-deep in a relationship that's starting to throttle us, it can be painfully hard for women (maybe especially for women) to disentangle themselves. I think many of us suffer from what I call the "disease of politeness." It can be deadly. When you combine that with our natural inclination toward hope, it can create an environment that isn't conducive to healthy boundaries. In their book *Safe People*, Drs. Cloud and Townsend unpack what hopeful creatures we humans are and how it's that very optimism that can keep us making excuses for all the heavy rocks we've found ourselves saddled with or hoping for change long past the point of healthy interactions:

> Sometimes simply hoping a person will change keeps us from the pain that we need to face. **Humans are incredible optimists when it comes to destructive relationships. For some reason we think that a person who is hurtful, irresponsible, out of control, abusive, or dishonest is going to change if we just love them correctly or more or enough.** We think that if we just let them know about their mistakes, or cry the blues, or get angry, that they will change. In short, we have hope, but it is hope that disappoints. In this scenario we use hope to defend ourselves against facing the truth about someone we love. We do not want to go through the sadness of realizing that they probably are not going to change. We don't want to accept the reality about who they are. So, we hope.[2]

There might be very few things more painful than a hope that disappoints. And it's the reason we often end up shouldering the burdens of our friends. Because we so badly want to see them healthy and fulfilled. Sometimes we're more invested in their well-being than they are. So what then? How do we love well without being dragged under by the weight of a friendship that's become too heavy and too unhealthy to keep carrying? How do we figure out when to keep trying and when it might be beyond our ability to fix things?

If ever there was a handbook on how to negotiate hard relationships and create fresh starts it's the Bible. "The chief theme of the entire Bible is reconciliation of unsafe relationships."[3] First, between us and God. Second, between us and the other people God has created. All throughout Scripture we see how God is relentless in His quest to remake us in His own image, often through our relationships with other people. Even the hard relationships. Sometimes especially through those. "This means that no relationship can be left without a struggle to negotiate and resolve problems, even the worst sins known to man. This is a far cry from the easy out that says, 'When I found that this person was unsafe, I left him.'"[4] Instead, God is in the business of "making everything new" (Rev. 21:5).

> **All throughout Scripture we see how God is relentless in His quest to remake us in His own image, often through our relationships with other people.**

This is what He modeled in His own relationships. He didn't give up on the hard, difficult frustrating ones. Instead, "He moved toward the relationship and became a facilitator of healing."[5] We see Him do this with Adam and Eve, Cain, Noah, Moses, Joshua, Rahab, David, Ruth, Peter, Paul, and on and on down through history to the bickering disciples, the early church, and all the way on to you and me and that coworker or PTA parent who makes you grind your teeth in irritation. God wants wholeness. God wants health. "His ideal was for people to stay in an unbroken relationship with him forever."[6]

"But things did not work out this way. People turned toward self-centeredness and away from God and his ways. And God was faced with the same dilemma that we are faced with in our relationships in a fallen world: Do I keep them, or do I move on?"[7] Every time I bump into another real-time, real-life example that God understands my life from the inside out, I'm surprised all over again. That He understands my tender scabs where friendships have cut and where I haven't been able to put things back together again. I'm amazed that the God of the universe and I share the same aching cry[8] that sometimes comes out as a whimper and sometimes as a gut cry of confusion, "I have been *hurt*" (Ezek. 6:9 NASB, emphasis mine).

If He's our role model in His hurt, then He can also be trusted as our role model in how to respond. Drs. Cloud and Townsend break down what God's consistent response to hurt has been throughout Scripture, down through history and into our own lives today:

We find that God (1) starts from a loved position, (2) acts righteously, (3) uses the community to transform us, (4) accepts reality and forgives us, (5) gives change a chance, and (6) is long-suffering.[9]

This list is not what I want to hear when I'm worn down by a difficult relationship. Instead, when I've done all that I believe I can, I have been known to tell God, "Well, I'm done," as I metaphorically dust off my hands and pat myself on the back for giving it such a good go. And I believe it. I'm done being patient and done trying to stand in her shoes and done trying to keep my heart open and done keeping my passive aggression in check and done with second, third, fourth chances.

And I believe I'm justified in feeling that way because just look, God! Look at all my hard work. Look at how I've cried and wrestled and felt like crap and gone back and tried again. And look where we *still* are. Obviously this has to be the end, yes? I mean, at some point we run out of trying. We run out of do-overs. We run out of interest or patience or conversations. At some point, surely, we both just get to be done.

But God, I have found, is stubborn. And He has stubbornly insisted in my life that there is no "done" when it comes to sacrificial love. There is only "more." This has been a shocking revelation to me. Shocking and, frankly, unwelcome. To discover that more would be expected of me. More listening. More changing. More bending. More willingness to be open. More awkward and more choosing to stay instead of cutting loose and quitting. God has kept me in some relationships way past what I would have considered to be the finish line. Way, uncomfortably, long past.

But He hasn't left me there alone. He's always been intimately involved and insanely patient. With me. And it has changed me. That's the kicker. It has changed *me* when I thought it was about changing the other person. It has taken apart all my assumptions about love and kindness and patience and that old-school word *long-suffering* and put them back together again in a picture that demonstrates how eternal God's patience is with me. With all of us.

I have found Him rabid in His ability to out-wait our selfishness, our stubbornness, our insistence on doing things our own way. He has walked me down the winding corridors of "more" miles and miles farther than I ever would have thought my legs or my heart could take. And it has been as rewarding as that first (and last) 5 km race I ran—grueling and profoundly satisfying. Being willing to let God work in me and through me for the sake of healing what was once a deeply unhealthy friendship has been nothing short of miraculous.

With that said, every difficult relationship I've tried to navigate hasn't had this miraculous outcome. I believe there have been several relationships that He just as tenderly, just as patiently walked me through to their season's end. Those relationships riddled with so much hurt and so many unhealthy habits that, instead of growing us both toward God, grew us away—like poison ivy that would choke the life out of the trees it winds itself around and sting anyone who tries to remove it.

Because in order to be agents of peace, of long-suffering, of long walks with a God who doesn't turn His back on relationship, we need to be healthy ourselves. We "need to be secure in our other relationships. Our support system needs to be intact."[10] Every time a relationship has been more toxic than I could possibly transform, I was either too young or too vulnerable or too unqualified to be able to make anything healthy out of that environment. Because some wounds need professional, tender counseling from those qualified to speak objectively into a raw and hurting person. In those cases, God has given me the protection of being able to grant forgiveness while simultaneously opening an exit for me to leave so there was still a chance to heal. Separately. Because forgiveness does not negate consequence, and change has to be chosen; it can't be forced.

For me one of those relationships started way back in middle school and graduated into greater and greater levels of dysfunction the older we got and the more I had the adult vocabulary to put into words how the relationship was hurting me. Especially at a time when my parents were distracted by hospitals and chemotherapy instead of teaching me about healthy boundaries.

I can't go back and fix those moments, so I try to go forward and distance myself from them. Knowing God is still walking with me, aching with me, understanding from the inside out the memories that can still disappoint, offering His Holy Spirit as a balm to soothe the wound and heal my mind.

Because while I have finally, truly, fully forgiven the actions that confused and hurt a vulnerable teenager, I know that forgiveness doesn't require friendship in order to be genuine. Forgiveness does not equal allowing unsafe people into our safe, inner circles.

"Boundaries are our spiritual and emotional 'property lines.' They tell us where we end, and where others begin. They help to keep good things in us, and bad things out. We take responsibility for what is ours, and not for what isn't. When we are clearly defined, we can carry our own loads, and we know when it's appropriate to help others with their burdens (Gal. 6:1–5)."[11]

> ### *Drawing safe boundary lines doesn't make you selfish, unChristian, or impolite; it makes you wise.*

Drawing safe boundary lines doesn't make you selfish, unChristian, or impolite; it makes you wise. It puts your hope in the right place—in the Christ who can actually transform and who won't disappoint (Rom. 5:5) instead of in our friends who can't help but fail us because, like us, they're human and flawed. Safe boundary lines and housing your hope in the right place will make you all the more capable of being a woman who is a safe place for her friends to unload their heavy burdens and trust that they will find encouragement in the shade of your friendship.

PART 3

WHAT *CAN* WE DO ABOUT IT?

"Here is a simple rule of thumb for behavior:
Ask yourself what you want people to do for you;
then grab the initiative and do it for them!" (Luke 6:31 MSG)

Okay, here it is—this is the secret to finding and keeping lasting friendships: become women who want to see the women around them flourish. They have a word for that in Hebrew—it's *shalom*. But not *shalom* like you might think. Not the overused, under-appreciated translation that we're so used to throwing around as the word *peace*—as in the opposite of conflict. Instead, this word is used more than two hundred times throughout Scripture in a radically more interactive way.

> *This is the secret to finding
> and keeping lasting friendships: become
> women who want to see
> the women around them flourish.*

The kind of shalom we're challenged to give to the people around us requires us to take an active interest in their physical and spiritual well-being. When you look up the various translations to understand how the word is used, *shalom* means caring about someone else's safety and soundness in body, welfare, prosperity, peace and contentment, friendship, and good health, to name just a few.[1] In addition to caring deeply about seeing conflict come to an end, shalom is passionately invested in seeking the well-being of others—other people, other places and cultures and neighbors.[2] It's about living into the Great Commission to become a blessing to the people around us—the "command for the children of Abraham to help the nations experience all the good gifts that God longs for them to enjoy."[3]

Shalom is a radical word that challenges us to wake up from our obsession with ourselves and instead start the deliberate choice of focusing on the people around us and desperately caring less about ourselves and more about their "health, prosperity, harmony, and wholeness. It means perfect welfare, serenity, fulfillment, freedom from trouble, and liberation from anything which hinders contentment."[4]

When Jesse sent his teenage son, David, out from his daily grind among their bleating flock of sheep to go and check on his brothers who were fighting at the front lines of King Saul's army, he was sending David to check up on their "shalom."[5] To see how they were doing physically—did they have enough to eat? As well as to see how they were doing spiritually—were they discouraged? How was their mood, their sense of hope, their faith in the outcome of the battle?

It's the same word Jesus used in His intimate sermon to His disciples when He told them, "Blessed are the peacemakers" (Matt. 5:9 ESV)—the "shalom makers." "It is a word bursting with energy. It mandates action and initiative."[6] Those who are invested, interested, and diligently working for the well-being of the people around them. "For they will be called sons of God" (Matt. 5:9). Because choosing this hard and deliberate course of being a peacemaker is to walk in the footsteps of the God-man, Jesus. The shalom maker who actively, deliberately stepped into every day of His life on earth choosing our well-being over His own even past the point when it cost Him His own life.

That's the gospel. We are at peace so we can *be* peace. We've been invested in so that *we* can invest.

So, what can you do to find safe, loving, engaged friends whom you can trust never to unfriend you? Become radically invested in the people around you. Take the initiative and become that kind of friend first. The kind of friend who:

1. Draws us closer to God.
2. Draws us closer to others.
3. Helps us become the real person God created us to be.[7]

Stop keeping score—who called who last, who owes who an e-mail or a play date or a lunch date—and start initiating. Friendship isn't something we passively receive. Friendship is something we actively do. It's a gift we offer for free, not a demand we make with a stamping foot.

> *Friendship isn't something we passively receive. Friendship is something we actively do. It's a gift we offer for free, not a demand we make with a stamping foot.*

It makes me think of my friend Crystal who is a fitness coach for a group of women she's gathered with gentleness and persistent encouragement. For a year I watched her labor of love, first on her own fitness journey as a full-time working mama, as she began the hard, deliberate work of making time for her health. And as she climbed that mountain, she invited others into the journey with her. I've never seen such guilt-free encouragement. Such determination to see the women around her grow stronger and more confident without any agenda of her own—other than simply being invested in their shalom—their wholeness, health, mind, body, and spirit. She has become a relentless cheerleader, and it's so endearing that it's what finally motivated *this* forty-something mom who spends hours hunched over a computer to believe that maybe she too could try to commit to fitness. Not out of guilt, but out of friendship.

Choosing to see people as holy reflections of the God who made them to be loved, cherished, and encouraged will change everything when it comes to how we interact with them. We can see people for what we can get out of them or for what we can give to them. We can see people as a source of influence, prominence, cool, or competition. Or we can see them as family, sisters, fellow pilgrims on this journey as we try to make sense of the everyday Tuesdays and Sundays and sadness and celebration. But we can't do both. We can either love them or compete with them. We can either champion them or condemn them. We can either accept them or try to change them. We can either love them for who they are or try to twist them into our own image. But we can't do both.

I want to be the kind of woman who makes other women feel welcome. Where they feel seen, valued, and safe. That means that whether or not we have close friends is entirely in our own hands. We simply have to be willing to start. Consider this section your friendship toolbox. It's a collection of all the ways you can initiate and then deeply invest in a friendship. It's not what you think. It's not the secret to finding friends who will never unfriend you. Instead, it's the key *to becoming the kind of woman who would never unfriend her friends.*

Start there. Because the woman who doesn't unfriend anyone on a whim, the woman who is a safe place for friendship, the woman who knows her own boundaries, the woman who is willing to go first, to be vulnerable, to offer guilt-free friendship—that's the woman who won't have to worry about being unfriended because she'll be the kind of friend we all want. And more importantly, she'll be the kind of friend we all *need.*

DARE TO GO FIRST AND BE UN-FINE

*"I know I am not fine, yet I do not want to cause
the ripples and waves that I would by letting anyone
know—at least anyone that knows me! 'Fine' is a
life preserver that I am too afraid to let go."* —Amanda[1]

IAM CONVINCED THAT THE shortest distance between strangers and friends is a shared story about our broken places. At the website where I've been the community manager for nearly a decade—www.incourage.me—we call this being willing to be "un-fine."

I am convinced that the shortest distance between strangers and friends is a shared story about our broken places.

Nothing is riskier or more vulnerable than cracking open the doors of our messy, guest-unready homes, let alone the doors of our actual lives. We get so used to being neatly packaged people and stories and families that we can forget how to be anything but "fine" when someone asks. Because, deep down, there are messes much messier than the dust bunnies or gritty dishes. There are fears and doubts and despair and broken places that cut so deep it takes the breath away.

And so we wrap them up in pretty packages of "I'm fine," like lipstick over trembling lips.

We smile at birthday parties and play dates and in our cubicles. We smile at church during worship and when the pastor shakes our hand. We nod and smile and say we're fine, the kids are fine, work is fine, marriage is fine, just fine, thanks for asking. And all the while there's this big, messy, gaping wound bleeding raw right through our perfectly fine outfit that we hope no one notices. All the while desperate for somebody to care enough to see.

> "Some days I feel so broken. Everything seems so
> messed up inside me. I know God is holding me tightly,
> but it would help to have friends I could be real with.
> Trouble is, I'm waiting for a sign that it's okay to open up,
> it's okay to stop pretending we're not all perfect." —E.G.[2]

For a long time I hid my messes. I was afraid of them. Afraid of what people would say and afraid that marriage and motherhood could feel so messy. So I just walked around with this bleeding gut wound, ignoring it and politely saying I was "fine" when anyone asked how I was doing. Like a Hello Kitty Band-Aid could hold together the disaster that was living behind my living room door and bleeding out my guts.

Fine is so dangerous, isn't it? Fine means the end of a conversation; the beginning of nothing. Now it's time for the battle cry that if Truth can set us free (John 8:32), it's best to start living in those places. Maybe going first and admitting our un-fine isn't a weakness; instead, it's a gift to the women around us who can finally exhale and admit their un-fine too.

Sure, it can be excruciating to admit our un-fine moments, but it's in those moments that people can actually *see* us to help us. We need people. We are a body. And if one part is all bashed up and bleeding, it hurts everywhere else.

All of us will be challenged and encouraged by friendship to let someone else into our "un-fine" places. "Research has found that girls who are more authentic in their friendships—by being open and honest about their true feelings, and even having conflicts—have closer, happier connections with each other."[3] Let's do it; let's be un-fine together, eh?

Band-Aids Don't Fix Bullet Holes

After a decade of living away from my homeland of South Africa, away from my family, my language, my favorite foods, and my people, we went home when I was pregnant with my first child, a son—Jackson. He would be my peace offering for having been gone for so long—the firstborn I would give birth to on South African soil.

It was supposed to be all our dreams come true. Living back in the land of the acacia tree and Hadida bird, where we were supposed to put down roots, find jobs easily, and introduce the first grandchild to all his many doting relatives.

Instead, Peter couldn't find consistent work, our finances didn't translate into a South African mortgage, and we ended up bringing our firstborn home to the tiny one-room cottage at the back of my parents' property, totally dependent on their generosity. The highs were like flying—all that family so close, so available for late-afternoon teas and birthday parties and babysitting and spoiling and helping with laundry and sharing Sunday lunches. But the lows were so desperate—a bank balance that evaporated and a credit line that shot sky high, a deepening sense of dependence and the inability to make it on our own. The dreaded feeling of having failed, of sinking and flailing and watching your dreams turn into stupid self-recrimination, and fear was suffocating.

Doubt and shame crept into every corner of our marriage. As the one with a work permit while Peter was still waiting on most of his documentation, I accepted a job offer and went back to work full-time while Peter stayed home with a newborn and his crushing PhD deadline. Finally, we moved into our own rental place, but we couldn't furnish it because all our belongings were still in storage in the States and we couldn't afford to ship them out.

Peter's days consisted of him sitting in the one small study with the fold-out desk table and the futon pillow on the ground (the frame was still in storage) and typing away at his computer while his son played in the next room with the nanny. Because Jackson would cry for Peter anytime he emerged, Peter hid in that one, five-hundred-square-foot room, alone, for months of doubtful writing. He had no nearby friends or potential for lunch dates because I needed our one car to commute to work.

We borrowed a farmhouse table from friends and set it up diagonally in the small living room to try and hide the fact that we were missing couches and throws and pillows and other signs of home. Jackson cried and woke up what felt like hundreds of times a night, and Peter and I quit sleeping; we also quit communicating, quit hoping it would get better until finally we wanted to quit each other.

But on Sundays we'd show up at church, and because we were both pastor's kids, we understood the drill and lived up to the role we were supposed to play. We dressed up real pretty, our baby was adorable, and I raised my hands in worship. But I stopped believing that God could hear me.

No one at church knew. Because we told no one. We never asked for prayer because that would have been admitting we'd failed. That we were failures. And that our marriage was hemorrhaging.

My family had no clue because we didn't tell them. Because depression had wrapped its sinuous fingers around our marriage. And depression lies and tells you that it's not worth fighting and that you're better off alone. So each of us stayed in the cell of our own making, and home was a dark place with little conversation, but when we emerged we were so good at switching into "happy new parents" mode that we faked it successfully for months.

Until Peter wouldn't fake it anymore and stopped coming to family gatherings. Jackson and I would venture out alone and play happy families with desperate enthusiasm to make up for the fact that we were alone.

We were at the botanical gardens one South African fall afternoon. The air was so clear and the light so tender that you could see the outline of joy that shimmered off the faces of the foster kids my parents loved with such ridiculous abandon. The picnic basket was huge. Kids and parents unfolded their Sunday-afternoon legs, laid down to be able to better reach the chips and dips and sandwiches, and everyone asked why Peter wasn't with us. And for the first time, even I didn't believe the excuses I was making up. They rang hollow in my ears and I felt defensive. But the questions kept coming until I answered them with tears and my own shredded admission, "I don't know!"

No one asked me anymore questions.

Later we spent hours walking the low-slung branches of the botanical garden's trees. Those trees bent over like hunchbacks and stretched out their arms for what felt like miles a few feet off the ground, perfect for walking the plank or daring yourself to try and stay upright on that ancient balance beam. I was the opposite of those trees with their deep ancient roots. I felt like a wisp of myself and that the light fall winds could have blown me away.

I was fine.

We were fine.

We flew home to the States to introduce the American family to our Jackson. And we never would have said a word about how desperate we were. Not a whisper.

It took my dad phoning my parents-in-law and outing our broken places, and then it took them coming alongside with gentle, tender first aid to get us to unlock the shame that had wrapped us up in so many broken secrets. It took much more than we had.

Because up until then all I had was my one Band-Aid that couldn't possibly hold together the open gut wound that bled awkwardly all the time. I walked around with this bullet hole through my insides and my one teeny Band-Aid that was hanging on for dear life while I mouthed over and over again the words, "Oh, thanks for asking, but we're fine. We're doing great." And all the while blood was gushing from the wound in my abdomen and no one seemed to notice.

But my father is a doctor and Peter's dad is a preacher, and together they tenderly helped us to look down and see our wounds, and then they began the hard process of cleaning and treating and bandaging us up.

It was awkward and embarrassing and un-pretty.

But it was also lavish, generous grace.

And a beginning. It was a beginning.

We found out afterward that my dad had called Peter's parents to tell them how worried he was about us. To tell them not to let us play the "fine" card. Not to believe us when we told everyone we were doing okay. It took our parents parenting us. Those were hard days. And harder were the conversations and confrontations. Because having pretended for so long, it hurt to peel back the layers. It made us defensive. It pulled scabs off barely contained wounds and it bled.

You might need counseling or therapy or a mentor or a new job or your parents to let you move back in for a season as you try to find your way out of the dark. For us it took a little of all the above as well as frank conversations admitting how un-fine we had become. There was a moment lying on a hotel bed between Pete's Aunt Marcia and Aunt Kim that I'll never forget. We were there to take all the cousins swimming in the pool and all the ladies had gone up to their room to change and let the baby rest. After I put him down, I plopped down on the bed and in that room surrounded by women who love me, suddenly there was no space anymore for my shame.

With Aunt Marcia on one side and Aunt Kim on the other, their warm selves warming up my terrified insides, it felt safe to share. To answer their quiet, tender questions about my husband and my marriage. And with tears leaking down my cheeks, laying sandwiched between grace and faith, I quietly admitted our un-fine, broken story. I stared at the hotel ceiling the whole time I talked, but I could feel their warm bodies cocooning me, and a girl can never have too many mamas loving her and investing in her health and her heart. After I shared mine with them in a hotel in downtown Moline, Illinois, it felt like the bleeding might finally stop.

Jesus is in the business of making all things new. And I've lived enough broken and loved enough friends through their own cracks to know that redeemed is not the same as fixed and that holes can still ache even when we're whole again. Death, divorce, loss, heartbreak—admitting them doesn't make us immune. Or cancel the loss. Or restore the missing.

But sometimes saying it out loud is an invitation to the God who already knows to meet us in our rips and tears and hold us together—often through the arms of our friends and family. The people who've heard us whisper, "Un-fine."

The Gift of Going First

After Peter and I started to put our marriage and our hope and our faith back together like an unexpected stained glass window that was much more beautiful because of all the broken bits and pieces, I swore I'd never hide behind "fine" again. We talked about it together. How we didn't ever want to go back to that place where hiding was more important than truth. How we didn't want to be tricked by the voice. The voice that comes in our darkest moments when we most need other people and tends to whisper the lie, "Why bother others? They'll see how weak you are. Where's your faith?"[4] Instead, we wanted to make peace with our un-fine places and admit that real life is always more beautiful than perfect pretending.

Then, four years and two moves later, our church in Virginia asked me to speak at the women's ministry monthly breakfast. I had no idea what to say or where to begin. All I could think to share was my long list of things I get wrong. On repeat. By this time, I'd finally learned not to be afraid of that list. I wasn't embarrassed by it. I didn't feel the need to hide it. It's a list of who I am and also who I'm not.

At thirty-seven, I had made peace with that combo. It no longer made me want to weep that I forget dentist appointments. Or that Micah had two cavities and we got all the way through the numbing before he couldn't take any more and we had to leave. Sure, they didn't get filled because he wouldn't keep his mouth open for the drill. But we showed up.

I wondered if I should tell them that the tumble dryer had been slowly dying for months and while I thought I should mention it to the landlord, I never actually got around to telling him till it was good and dead and churning out stone-cold wet clothes.

There was also a birthday party I had promised Micah back in December that still hadn't happened, and then there was the week I invited people to Zoe's first birthday party for the wrong month, for goodness' sakes.

I remembered that for two days (and one night), a Diaper Genie sat outside our front door. Don't ask. I sound like a woman stuck together with chewing gum and twine some days. But on the inside I'm a lot more solid. There's this growing sense of who I am through Jesus' lenses. Far, far from perfect. But deeply and profoundly loved. So thoroughly loved that my places where I get everything wrong aren't as terrifying to me anymore.

So even though I wondered if God would give me something super spiritual to say that Saturday, it seemed like He just shook His head and told me to keep doing at our women's breakfast what I'd been practicing in real life—open the door to your mess and let other people in.

So that Saturday morning found me standing in front of a lovely group of women and an even lovelier array of cinnamon crunch bagels sharing how desperately inept I'd felt when it came to mothering a daughter. How for years I attended a church where I didn't know anyone beyond "fine." And how my new strategy for making friends was going to be sharing more than they're expecting to hear.

I want to be a radical truthteller when it comes to how hard motherhood is and also how holy.

I want to admit the days I am absolutely, 100 percent NOT fine.

I want to give the gift of going first by admitting my own struggles so other women can finally be comfortable asking for encouragement in theirs.

Friendship lives beyond the margins of Facebook or blog posts, church bulletins or smartphones. Friendship cups real hands around paper cups of coffee. Friendship can see when your mascara runs. Believe me when I tell you that we need those friends. We need to pack up our excuses and join that Bible study or moms group or coffee hour or book club or running team that we've been meaning to for months now.

Or maybe all we need to do is tell the truth when someone asks, "How are you doing?"

I promise it won't be perfect.

Friendship with skin will let you down. It will likely hurt you sometimes. But it will laugh with you, not at you, over the everyday bits and pieces that make us real. So these days, I'm going all in. Random Diaper Genie outside the front door and all.

It's Okay to Need Help

This past week our family was so sick we couldn't see straight. It was a seventy-two-hour marathon of toilets and buckets and bowls, and the laundry running round the clock on repeat. One by one I watched each kid succumb until it was finally my turn. Pete was the last man standing, until he wasn't.

It was brutal.

We were shaken, and when my boys could finally straggle their way back to school, they looked relieved to be leaving behind the scene of the crime. I was left with a still-sick husband, what felt like a hundred more loads of laundry to go, and the desperate urge to text my mother-in-law, begging her to get on the next flight out and rescue me from being a grown-up.

Some days it's hard to scrape yourself up off the floor.

On days like that it's almost shocking when someone offers to help.

Because on days like that you're so undone you don't recognize yourself in the mirror.

The competent version of yourself got lost around 5:00 a.m. three days back, and you aren't sure how to take the next step forward. You just keep spraying down the counters and moving cups of water from one place to another.

You forget to brush your hair.

You're still too nervous to brush your teeth.

You look at the wreckage of your house and it's all too much, and instead you sit down on the carpet and stare into space. Around you the world seems to keep pace with the news and the headlines and the deadlines, but in your four walls, time has crawled to a standstill. And when the lady from the rental agency knocks at the door for your annual inspection, you stare at her in confusion because you forgot that everything outside your house hadn't stopped to take pity on what's happening inside.

You need to buck up, you tell yourself.

You need to get it back together.

You need to clean the upstairs bathroom floor. Again.

And you need to check your messages.

I'm in the minivan—with all its discarded innards spilling in a confused chaos of shame out of the car and into the parking lot of my daughter's preschool—when I get the message.

A friend, a fellow mama and writer, is throwing stew in the Crock-Pot at 9:00 a.m. and wants to know if I'd like her to drop half of it off for dinner at 6:00 p.m.?

I don't even hesitate.

I pick up the phone to reply, "No thanks, we're fine."

And then I remember how it's only when we admit our un-fine moments that people can actually get to us to help us.

It's one thing to write that; it's something else to actually live it.

I just sit in the car with something sticky underneath my shoe and consciously breathe in and out. And in and out again.

Then I pick up the phone and just say four words, "Thank you, yes please."

I text her my address and then put my head down on the steering wheel and cry. Because comfort can undo you. Kindness can unglue you.

Because the biggest kind of self-deception is for us to think we've got our lives under control. We're all just one stomach bug, one bad report card, one month of missed work, one negative interview, one lost wallet away from losing all the bits and pieces of our lives we hold on to with such tight fists.

And sometimes you sit in a minivan with both hands wide open and palms up to the sky and just whisper, "Thank You, thank You" through your tears and snotty nose. And Jesus reminds you, again, that you are not in control. It may seem like He's asleep in the boat, but it's not because He doesn't care. It's because He's so deeply confident the Father is in control.

I've eaten Angela's stew for the last four meals now.

Dinner the first night. Hot, chewy, chunky bits of meat and pieces of potato and carrots. Rice on the side. The kids inhaled it. Then I ate it for breakfast and lunch the next day and lunch again today. My eyes well up every time I open that Tupperware lid. It's why I keep eating it. Because this is the totally, uncomplicated gift of friends who aren't afraid of our un-fine. Because this is what grace tastes like.

Totally underserved. And totally fulfilling.

The Truth Will Set You Free to Make Friends

It was seven months since the last baby was born and I was still fighting with my jeans.

She was wearing hers like a perfect fit, and I couldn't help but say what I was really thinking, *Man, you look great. You just look so good. How'd you do that? How'd you get back to the pre-baby shape so quick?*

And I didn't know what I was expecting. But I was not expecting her to say what she was really thinking. I didn't expect that at all.

"Stress. A lot of stress. I was running and then I got too busy and now I eat once a day and grab a chocolate bar. It's not good. But it is what it is."

I was floored right there in the back of church before we headed out to lunch together. I had been so used to hearing the polite answer, I think I'd forgotten how comforting the real one is.

It's powerful when a friend steps out from behind fine and looks you in the eyes.

Christy gives me friendship instead of fine. She gives me freedom to share my washer-packed-up, toilet-backed-up, kids-all-been-sick-all-week, some-times-I-think-I'm-losing-my-mind, opposite-of-fine answers too. It's like remembering how to exhale. When you're reminded that it actually doesn't come easy all the time to everyone. That fine is usually an awkward diminishing of the truth. Grown-up camouflage.

> *It's powerful when a friend steps out from behind fine and looks you in the eyes.*

Karine e-mailed me encouragement, and I was getting ready to e-mail her back when I picked up the phone instead. It took me awhile to find it. I always lose it under books and kindergarten reading assignments that somehow get left to the last moment.

But when I did find it, it was worth it. Her voice was laced with warmth and understanding when I told her how my "office" is fighting the onslaught of miniature 18-wheelers, stuffed dogs, and Legos. I sat in an island of sunshine adrift in a Tuesday afternoon of upheaval, and she didn't flinch when I told her I don't feel fine. Instead, she told me about her own day of doctor's tests and homeschooling and undone dishes.

We came out of hiding together.

The baby slept while I listened to Karine's stories and laughed so hard that I started to feel normal again. And when we were done talking—when I'd started dinner and fought with Jackson over hot dogs and told Micah to take off his shoes—I opened my inbox and found she'd sent me a postscript to our conversation. She'd sent pictures of her everyday chaos. Kitchen, living room, and hallway that looked like the familiar semi-war zone of my own home. I smiled, or maybe I cried.

Jesus said, "If you hold to my teaching, you are really my disciples. Then you will know the truth, and the truth will set you free" (John 8:31–32 NIV).

A few minutes later, I went back to the hot dogs and the son who insists on trying to feed Zoe, and my chest wasn't quite so tight. Coming out of hiding is good for the soul. It's essential for friendships. So on Tuesday night we went out to dinner. We rearranged schedules and asked good men to watch our many kids. We planned times and which mall we'd meet at. Karine and Connie and Christy and Janice and Lisa and I sat down for two hours over cheesecake and conversation—and no one wasted time being fine.

CREATE (IMPERFECT) TIME AND SPACE TOGETHER

"I think behind our Internet communication are many, many women craving one-on-one, face-to-face time with each other."
—Kathy[1]

FOR MANY OF US women, I think our craving for connection is in direct conflict with our obsession with perfection. If our houses need to be tidy, if all the laundry needs to be put away and all the floors need to be swept or vacuumed and the candles lit before we're comfortable inviting someone over, we'll never be up for it. Because "ain't nobody got time for that."

That standard of entertaining means that we'll be too busy cleaning and prepping to remember that friendship works best when we show up just the way we are. Putting too much pressure on our appearances—whether in the mirror or in our houses—means that we'll get tired of all that frustration and busyness, and we'll collapse on the couch and shrug and say, "It's just not worth it!"

Because it isn't. Because friendship shouldn't equal entertaining. No, friendship should look more like yoga pants—comfortable, old, worn in, and stained. I think we can do it. I think it's easier than we think. But it starts with our willingness to open the door whether we're prepared or not. It starts with admitting that our quest for perfection is a gift to no one. Real friendship will insist on getting past that front door of perfection until it finds that closet or drawer that's stuffed full of our junk and it will insist on opening it.

There is no such thing as perfect. There is especially no such thing as perfect women, parents, waistlines, homes, kids, or friends. Perfect doesn't exist. Perfect is not an attainable goal. Perfect is merely a street sign at the intersection of impossible and frustration in never-never land. Perfect will leave you lonely.

But friendship teaches us that perfect is rarely as interesting and never as satisfying as real. If we want lasting friendships, we need to learn what real looks like. What real-time friendships that have been carved out of imperfect chunks of time in imperfectly curated spaces look like. In other words, this is friendship that happens while sitting on the carpets that have a layer of dust or crushed Cheerios and in between negotiating kid squabbles or term paper deadlines or right there at the curb while you're picking up your mail. This is the kind of friendship we've all got time for and that we can all make space for. Because this kind of friendship says that you and your house are both welcome just the way you are.

The Size of Your House Has Nothing to Do with the Size of Your Hospitality

My childhood is full of memories of dropping in on neighbors. If we happened to be driving down your street, my mom would pull over and we'd rush out of the car and through the front door, barely pausing to knock. It was a time of open doors and flexible ideas when it came to what a "visit" meant. It didn't require an invitation and certainly not an RSVP. We called all our friends' parents "Aunty" or "Uncle," and their houses were our houses. I don't remember a single time we called before dropping by. My mom was always picking up strays after church on Sunday, whether or not she'd especially prepared something special to serve.

But suggest an unplanned visit to someone today and watch them break out in hives. I've felt that itchy, scratchy discomfort myself. The panic that someone might catch me right there in the middle of my everyday life, with hair pulled back in a mess and still sporting my pajama pants. If I'm being honest, I've even sweated the planned visits. I admit I like the perfectly planned setting, food, kid behavior, and a visit that has a set start and end time.

For years I would have described myself as a "reluctant renter." We were married seventeen years before we bought our first house. And one of our longest rentals was small, grubby, and had faux bricks that constantly fell off the kitchen walls, and carpets that, well, let's just say back then we had three kids under the age of six and leave the rest up to your imagination.

For years my small, terribly imperfect house stunted my hospitality.

Before that, I'd always loved to have friends over. I'm not awesome with a glue gun and I do not have any real furniture-arranging mojo, but I'm generally comfortable in my own skin. And I love lingering over the last of the hot chocolate with friends and leaving the dishes for later. Give me girlfriends, church friends, grandparents, aunts, uncles, or cousins—I love to have them in my space.

But my space had shrunk in that rental and it turns out my hospitality had shrunk right along with it. I didn't realize quite how much until our South African cousins surprised us with the news they were going to be coming through the DC area and were so excited to come and visit—and hopefully stay—with us.

I was elated for five minutes before the wave of embarrassed disappointment hit.

The teeny living room, three bedrooms, and one bathroom with the aqua blue bathtub and broken toilet seat all flashed through my mind. Then there was the not-so-small matter that we only had four dining room chairs and no guest bedroom. An inflatable mattress and sofa pillows were the best we had to offer overnight guests.

Five of them and five of us in our house seemed like a recipe for hostess hyperventilation. (Insert entertaining-in-a-small-house nightmares here.) So I was relieved when they said they'd be happy to stay at a hotel. And astonished when my husband e-mailed them back and insisted they stay with us.

I was incredulous. I pointed out the obvious. Our. House. Is. Small.

Turned out, however, Peter wasn't limited by the size of our house. Because he had big hospitality in mind.

He said we should give them our master bedroom and we'd take the inflatable mattress in the playroom, even if it was only for a night. The kids could camp out on mattresses and sofa cushions in the living room. He was determined that our homesick boys would get a full dose of family. Sleepovers included.

For dinner, we made a taco fiesta buffet and everyone ate anywhere they were comfy. We put our best sheets on the bed and fluffed up our favorite pillows for them. The boys rolled out their blankets and stuffed toys and plotted games and snacks and stories.

In the five years we lived in that tiny, quirky, run-down house, it never felt as big as it did the week our family visited us. I learned that big hospitality has nothing to do with the size of the house. That big hospitality is a matter of the heart and not the architecture. That fellowship and friendship are never limited by the number of chairs available. And that the person who suffers the most from hiding behind closed doors and perfectly planned visits and insisting that we can't have anyone over until we're in a bigger house or have a cleaner carpet or a tidier backyard is me.

In the last seven years, I've become painfully aware of how desperate women are for meaningful female friendships. But because the ideals of what a home should look like before you have people over have sky-rocketed with the rise of HGTV and Pinterest, we all suffer from stage fright at the thought of inviting people over into our real lives. Home blogger and anti-perfection advocate, Myquillyn Smith, affectionately known as "the Nester," writes in her book *The Nesting Place*, "We like to tell ourselves that we are insisting on perfection for the betterment of those around us. But really, insisting on perfection is a self-centered act. Because the irony is that giving up on perfection isn't a failure. It's a gift."[2]

If women were willing to let their friends into a version of their homes and their lives that was unstaged, it could start a revolution. A revolt against the impossible standards of having to stuff all our junk behind closed closet doors that have first been perfectly, beautifully painted and then artfully distressed. Instead, what if we let our friends see our dust bunnies and the unfinished parts of our homes and our lives so that they could feel less awkward doing the same. I love a tidy, beautiful home as much as the next girl, but I'm done being held hostage by perfection—in both my house and my life.

The best four hours I've had since we moved to our new house were spent with Lisa one afternoon. My former neighbor and neat-freak friend knows me through and through. And she's as comfortable with my casually messy ways as I am with her fabulously tidy house. We've learned to lean in closer than what our homes look like on the outside, all the way in to get close views of each other's inside lives. And the day before she was supposed to come over, I frantically tried to restore order to the landscape of devastation that is the bedroom my sons share. And I had one hand full of misplaced Legos and the other on the handle of the vacuum cleaner when I suddenly asked myself out loud, "What am I doing? It's Lisa who's coming over tomorrow!" And I immediately stopped my manic cleaning and went to make a cup of tea.

Because Lisa's known me for years. There's nothing I can dress up for her that she hasn't already seen. And more than that, Lisa loves to clean. She's my very own personal Monica. So I laughed when I called and told her what to expect when she arrived. And she laughed in return and arrived the next day with her kiddo in tow and we moved our conversation into the boys' room.

Then we spent the next four hours talking and cleaning. It was time and space shared together with total honesty and also cleaning spray, mops, and wet rags. It was the very essence of our friendship. And as I looked over at her voluntarily sorting the boxes of my boys' Legos "for fun," I thought my heart might bust wide open it was so deeply loved and known in that moment.

Lisa gets me and I get her, and it's not about the state of our houses but the state of our friendship that makes both the mess and the pretty so equally comfortable.

Create Imperfect Time Together

The minivan-driving years are so exhausting and so full of our kids' schedules, it's hard to make time to invest in friendships, let alone find new ones. But I think that another part of the problem might be that we judge the state of our friendships by how many friends we have and how much time we have to spend with them. Whether we're minivan-driving moms or college-aged students or grandmas long since retired, we can all fall prey to thinking that it's the number of women we know or connect with that will fill up our loneliness.

Truthfully, I think that, "the more friends the better" is the Facebook definition of friendship. In my real life it's the depth and regularity of the relationships that fill me up and tell me, "This is my friend." An hour with one friend who knows all my messy story can fill up all my empty places more fully than a whole day spent with a roomful of shiny acquaintances.

I was sitting across a cup of tea in Christie's one-hundred-year-old farmhouse when I told her, "I didn't realize how lonely I was last year." She's known me since the days I swore I'd never be interested in being anyone's mother. And this afternoon our daughters are curled up in the last of the sunlight on the sofa together.

An hour with one friend who knows all my messy story can fill up all my empty places more fully than a whole day spent with a roomful of shiny acquaintances.

We've been coming to visit them a weekend here and there over the last four years since they moved to Pennsylvania and were back within driving distance from us. Christie and I walked out to the beds of compost that will become her flower garden and pulled up two chairs in her gardening shed with the wind blustering outside, the smell of manure in the air, and our kids hanging off a zip line. We sat in that imperfect setting and talked and talked and talked. I used to make lists before we would get together to make sure we didn't miss catching up on anything. I'm always so hungry for conversation with someone who knows me and is interested in me beyond a witty tweet or Facebook update.

We talked for hours. The wind kept slamming the doors and windows on the gardening shed, kids hollered from a distance, and we kept right on talking. I hadn't realized how much I had been needing to say, to process out loud, until someone was willing to listen without rush or deadlines. There were hurts I hadn't stopped to pay attention to. There were holes in my faith that I needed someone to stand in alongside me. There were doubts I needed someone to acknowledge.

One of the ways our world of the fast and furious Internet hurts us is that so often our schedules and attention spans don't have enough time to give each other uninterrupted hours of conversation. We will starve on a diet of conversations limited to 140 character tweets, text messages, or Facebook quips. We need soul food conversations. The kind that don't cut you off because they have another meeting to run to. The kind that lingers.

That weekend Christie gave me what Dr. Leslie Parrott calls in her book *Soul Friends* the "extravagant gift of time and undivided attention."[3] It's a love language that runs deep for me. I'm guessing, if you're a woman, then it runs deep for you too.

We need to talk and talk and talk till we are all filled up from the gift of having someone else listen. Soul friends pay attention to what you're saying, not to what time the clock says it is. Soul friends listen as long as it takes to make you feel heard. Soul friends aren't in a hurry to get to the point or to check you off the list. Soul friends are more interested in the state of your heart than the state of your house.

It's taken me years of these kinds of conversations for the truth to permeate my paranoia about my house or my hair or my life—true friends will always make time and space for each other. Period. It's how our "Tuesday night girls" were born.

Every Tuesday night for years before our move I met up with a group of women. Sometimes in room 108 at church and every other week at Panera. We were suckers for the broccoli cheddar soup. Connie always wore the most beautiful jewelry. And Christy sometimes brought baby Taylor.

We ate and talked and sometimes we laughed so hard that we forgot to be self-conscious. No one left with an empty belly or heart. We ate up friendship like so many cinnamon crunch bagels. Hugged Mrs. Santiago so tight and heard Carol share about her journey into the heart of the heart of motherhood. That and learned what nail "schlacking" is. Jessica amazed us by turning vegan and sticking to it. Sometimes my hair was washed and other times it wasn't. Sweat pants were always welcome. But Shawna would always rock the six-inch heels. They were my people. They knew about the impending new puppy and the week of diarrhea the four-year-old put us through. And when they asked me how I was doing, I knew I was going to need to come up with more than "just fine."

These are the moments that friendships are built on. If we don't grab them with both hands, we're missing out on the deeply satisfying state of being known by someone else. I'm no longer in the same town, but I still keep in touch with almost every one of those Tuesday night girls. We text; we send voice messages; we meet up at odd snatched moments when our paths happen to cross. And we insist on telling each other how we're really doing. We make totally imperfect time for each other.

There was a moment, though, a moment I would take back if I could. It was a selfish moment before our move. It was a split-second moment when I wasn't willing to make time for one of those women. I remember it with a knot in my stomach. It was a night when I was tired and our kids were being wild and unruly after a late-night church event and all I wanted was to wrangle everyone back into the minivan, to home, and to bed. I wanted my shoes off and my hair down and my comfy pants on. And as I was cutting through the church sanctuary and the small knots of people still standing around chatting, I kept my eyes down so that I wouldn't have to stumble into conversation with anyone.

I wove my way through the chairs trying to get to my kids and spotted one of my Tuesday night girls with her back to me and her hand on her cane. Without even giving it a second thought, I backtracked around her so that I wouldn't have to pause to talk. So that I wouldn't have to give up a second of my stupid, selfish time to a friend who lived by herself in a small room with her cats and her passion for beautiful, colorful necklaces and who came out every Tuesday night because she was so hungry for company.

I backtracked around my friend, and just a few weeks later she had a stroke that she never recovered from. And she died before there was a chance for any more nights together. It was a small, invisible moment that she didn't even know I stole from her, but steal it I did. And it was the last time I saw her alive. I saw only her back because my tired, selfish heart avoided a friend when it should have given the gift of its own time and presence. I know better. And I have to live with that memory. How I was a Scrooge with time—the gift that doesn't even belong to me, but that was gifted by my God who spoke hours and minutes into being the moment He set the sun and the moon in the sky.

I stood at her memorial service, though, and I got to bear witness to the generous way she had spent her life. I got to hear from person after person about how she'd poured herself into each one of them. They laughed and cried, and we all sang our hearts out in memory of a woman who was quirky and beloved and I loved her too. And she wasn't perfect and she knew I wasn't either, and now I get to carry her in my heart where she reminds me that giving people our time is an act of radical generosity. It's countercultural to refuse to utter those three words we say without even thinking, *I'm too busy*. I don't want to be too busy. I want to be available.

I'm a realist; I know it's impossible to be available to everyone. But to the few God has trusted me with? The friends who do life with me and my people? I owe them my availability.

It's countercultural to refuse to utter those three words we say without even thinking, I'm too busy. I don't want to be too busy. I want to be available.

The One Thing You Have to Be Willing to Do If You Want Friends

Since Christie and I sat in that shed and I sat in my circle of Tuesday night girls and I sang at a funeral, we've had a lot of guests pass through our conveniently-located-right-outside-DC house. But right up to our most recent move, my desire to host people with the carefree abandon of my childhood continued to go head-to-head with my desperate self-consciousness about the cramped size of our rental house.

How the size of our house felt like it had stunted the size of my life.

How pockmarked our yard was with the holes of busy boys, the mud they'd lovingly smeared as "cement" all over the back pavement, the rakes and hammers and shovels and old gloves they'd forgotten in piles around their precious work site that I didn't have the heart to complain about.

How we only had four dining room chairs and how the table was littered with markings that even a Mr. Clean Magic Eraser couldn't seem to remove. And how inevitably my kids would open the hamster cage and bring him over to the table right as I was trying to serve the meal.

It used to give me profound waves of panic. Because there's nothing like seeing your house through someone else's eyes to realize the carpet might actually be beyond cleaning. Or that the toilet seat with the one loose side that never bothers you is an embarrassment when you think about someone else using it. And that if you don't warn the friend helping you load the dishwasher, she won't know that you can only pull it out so far before it comes completely off the rails and glasses and bottles bounce foolishly off the tracks.

There was a weekend when one of my oldest friends and her good man who had been deployed more than he'd been home the last few years and their three kids came to visit. They came several days earlier than we expected. And there it was. The choice.

Panic or delight.

Fear of appearances or fully opening my arms to one of my favorite friends.

Picking up the backyard or inviting her boys to join the well-loved chaos.

Stressing the stains or surrounding ourselves with toys, kids, and enough time to catch up.

Frantically planning something to cook or ordering pizza and slicing a watermelon.

After five years in that small house with all the brown paneling, I had learned a lot about big hospitality. No matter how much you clean or remodel or move or rebuild, hospitality will always be more a matter of the heart than the architecture. And your guests will only feel as comfortable in your house as you feel in your own skin. And there's no shame in paper plates if they're heaped high with delight in each other's company. And kids are great role models when it comes to the un-self-conscious art of explaining the ins and outs of each other's toilets.

And no one ever did actually die of embarrassment.

But missing out on community is a kind of dying, and what if I'd said no to catching up on two decades and three kids since we shared a dorm together?

So, it's later, after we've said a hundred good-byes in the space of ten minutes and after the boys have all agreed they'd like to be brothers and next-door neighbors and after I've wiped down sticky counters, chairs, and sofas that I discovered that dirty pot in the microwave.

I stood and stared at it. Looked like it was from yesterday's tacos. "Pete," I asked over my shoulder. "Did you know there's a pot in the microwave?"

There's a pause before he answers.

And then his laughter rolls back from the couch with his words, "Yeah, I guess that's where I hid it before they came over."

I wonder if my mom ever did that? Shoved dirty dishes in the stove or a cupboard? I don't remember us having a microwave. But on Sunday afternoons in South Africa there were always watermelons bopping in the swimming pool. It was to keep them cool till they could be split for dessert. But to us kids they were just a challenge to ride, to raft, to water polo between ourselves until a grown-up finally noticed and yelled to quit it before we turned the insides into pure pulp.

Sunshine on the watermelons and their green-striped skins and our shoulders and legs all gangly and growing up living large on the hospitality of our parents. I can still feel the water running down my back from wet hair as we stood dripping around the table under the thatch roof pergola as Dad cut into the melons slice after juicy slice.

We'd stand and bite and suck and spit seeds, and there were always more people than chairs. My mom could make an ordinary afternoon an event. So much goodness dripping down our chins and still feeding my memory tonight—twenty-three years later—in a small rental house in Northern Virgina. It's a long way from my Southern Cross childhood and that swimming pool in Pretoria.

And I think about how Mom used to burn the beans because she wasn't paying attention, or run out of mashed potatoes because the kids helped themselves to too much, or flip the brown sofa cushion over where it had split a gut right open.

But she always opened the door. She always pulled out one more chair. Kids were always included in the charades, the impromptu Bible lessons, the cleaning up. And there was always watermelon for dessert.

Today, Sunday afternoons are messy at our house. And I like them that way. We've usually let the weekend play around us with all its Legos and dolls and light sabers and blanket forts and leftover pizza. We've let the dishes pile up and a pile of, well, everything really, accumulate in the boys' room. At least one of our children is wearing only underpants. And Pete and I usually nap, then drag our bedheads up and back into the land of the living when Zoe wakes us up. The late-afternoon sun pours in the windows across the brown sofas, showing every single spot or stain or trail of old milk.

It is very hard to open the door when someone knocks on afternoons like that.

When someone arrives without calling or planning, simply showing up to say hi or to ask the boys over for a play date or to drop off hand-me-down clothes for Zoe, the last thing I want is for them to catch me right in the middle of my real life.

There's panic and a profound desire to hide. Then the reflex to kick everything into the boys' room and try to wedge the door shut. To fix my hair, rush on a layer of makeup, kick off my mismatched socks.

There's an instinct to hide who I am at my messiest behind a volley of words, excuses, explanations for why the backyard looks like the place where toys go to die. How I'd been watching Peter and Jackson swordfight their way across the dirt and in between the discarded plastic swords that were everywhere except in the toy bin. How I'd cracked open the window to yell that swords must be put away before new games are started, but instead just stood and watched the two of them whack and laugh their way across the sunny afternoon.

But here's the thing. If I wait for my house or my life to be perfect before inviting someone into it, I might never let anyone come through the door.

A few girlfriends and I were discussing this, and we talked about how we want to let each other deep into the layers of our real lives, selves, fears, hopes, and desperate prayers. It seemed fitting that at the time I was still tired from a late flight the night before, with hair thrown up on my head and no makeup, no ChapStick, no camouflage.

If I wait for my house or my life to be perfect before inviting someone into it, I might never let anyone come through the door.

We get to choose this kind of intimacy. Or not.

Shauna Niequist says, "You can decide that every time you open your door, it's an act of love, not performance or competition or striving. You can decide that every time people gather around your table, your goal is nourishment, not neurotic proving. You can decide."[4]

I never feel more vulnerable than when a friend is stepping over the threshold and picking her way in between the layers of chaos that say, "We live here. And we've never got it perfect." I still prefer the days they drop by when candles are lit and carpets vacuumed. But if I believe what I say about friendship, then that includes the messy days. The ones where I've been too tired to catch up on much of anything.

It includes welcoming my people into the nooks and crannies of my ordinary and remembering not to be ashamed. Remembering that to become real, friendship more often than not requires becoming comfortable with the snapshots of life often taken at an unflattering angle. I love how my friend Sharone puts it: "I don't care about the good pictures, really. The world can have your avatars. Give me the pictures you'd never want anyone to see. The things that are unpublishable. Let's be just us, in the space between photos."[5]

So I open my front door, wearing the jeans that always fall down without a belt. And my hair pulled back in a ponytail. The red shirt I've just discovered has a long thready pull. And no makeup.

My son complains about his afternoon, and my daughter's hair looks like she's slept in a haystack for two days. There's a pile of yesterday's dinner dishes in the sink, and a load of laundry chugging around in cycles. I haven't had time to force the boys to pick up their room yet, but you're welcome to sit down with feet up on the ottoman cover I just washed, again. Only this time it was because of orange, drippy, ice cream stains.

Because I want you here. Whether I'm ever perfectly ready or not. I want you.

Just the way you are. Which will likely mean most days, I must open the door just the way I am too.

EXPERIENCE GOD TOGETHER THROUGH SHARED SADNESS AND CELEBRATION

"Recently I had a woman I had only just gotten to know through my Bible Study invite herself over to sit and listen to my own story of grief. Her presence and tears for my loss meant so much more than anything else anyone had offered me in my grief."
—Anna[1]

MAYBE THE MOST INTIMATE, radical thing we can do for our friends is to show up. To show up like Jesus did—in person, willing to experience life with the community around Him. Giving our friends the same gift Jesus did—the gift of our presence. To show up and do one of two things—"Rejoice with those who rejoice; weep with those who weep" (Rom. 12:15). Cry the ugly cry or celebrate with whooping and hollering and confetti.

> **Maybe the most intimate, radical thing we can do for our friends is to show up.**

The radical thing about prayer is that it can accompany both—both grief and celebration. Jesus models what it looks like to invite God into both. To watch God participate fully, wholly, without holding any part of Himself back from both of these deep and primal emotions. Emotions modeled on the Godhead Himself. Jesus wasn't imitating us when He wept or rejoiced; instead, we imitate the God in us every time we experience the deep swell of emotions He created to run through our veins and beat in our hearts on earth as it is in heaven.

Jesus lived the whole arc of the human emotional spectrum—from weddings to funerals. He announced His public ministry at a wedding (John 2:1–11). Dancing, love, laughter, and passion. And in Jewish culture seven days of unmitigated joy, of food, of family, of telling stories, and of catching up on life and celebrating.

But He also stood outside the tomb of a friend as close as a brother and wept His broken tears alongside friends and strangers, believers and doubters (John 11). Wept with them for the brother who had died. Who had been dead days before He even arrived on the scene. Wept even while knowing He had the power to raise Lazarus. That He *would* raise Lazarus just moments later. Wept because friendship shares an emotional DNA, and His was tied up with Mary and Martha, and He entered fully into their grief. Their joy was His joy; their sorrow was His sorrow. He carried all of it. He opened His human heart and let it all pour in. He walked into their lives and didn't hold back feeling the full range of all that they lived and loved and hoped and despaired.

When we've run out of words, when we're beside ourselves with the pain that we're watching our friends go through, we can follow His example and give them the gift of our presence, our tears, our sorrow. We can always give them that.

When we don't know what to write in that card or note, when we can't figure out the perfect gift for that promotion or new baby or art show or book release, we can give the thing that's even better—we can give ourselves. We can give our grinning, applauding delight. We can give without holding back even a scrap of ourselves. We can give till their joy is our joy, and we're so full of it that it fills up the spaces between us with the Holy Spirit who builds new bridges to the hearts of the people with whom Jesus has trusted us.

And when words fail on the dark days, when the nightmares have crawled up into the light of day and blocked out the sun, He will intercede with "wordless groans" (Rom. 8:26 NIV), and we just need to be willing to let Him. To let Him groan through us on behalf of our friends. God and grief and joy and the marriage of all the emotions that make us the most human and the most obviously created in His image. A good Father, the kind of father that John Blase describes as having one primary role, "to be there, on-site, in the scene, to keep the fear at bay . . . to protect simply by presence."[2]

We give this to our friends when we're willing to experience God with them through their joy and also through their grief. We become ministers of the Holy Spirit in those moments on that holy ground. And it's the most intimate combination of experiencing both friendship as well as God, together. For He created and He modeled both. And we would do well to take Him at His word and His example and trust that this is the way to bless our friends. By giving them the gift of our presence, our snorting laughter and snotty tears, right there in the shelter of His own holy presence.

Be Willing to Carry Each Other's Pain

It was a Sunday morning five years ago. I can still picture it. They're all there. They stand tight around her, each touching a shoulder, an arm, her back—any part of her they can reach. There's Rema with the silver-gray hair who always sends me a personal card when I miss a Sunday. There's Janice who teaches with such courage and conviction. Connie has a house in the woods that rings us around with campfire smoke and hospitality, and who comes to visit me and brings chocolate cake. I don't know if I ever remembered to give her back the plate. Bunni who has as many children as there are kids in the church, and Trudy who limps forward with the cast still on one leg to reach out a hand to join her sisters. Denise—the teacher my sons love—has both hands raised, reaching down only to wipe her face now and again.

They are praying for the woman with the paper-thin skin.

I know that woman. I recognize that skin, unnaturally delicate, stretched tight over cheekbones. The fever-flush glow to it and the story it tells of a course of treatment almost as bad as the disease. Eighteen years ago that was my mom's skin and my mom's scarf-wrapped head and my mom's eyes sunken low into the face of a woman who sees the world in the perspective of eternity. Today the symptoms belong to Peggy.

The women are praying for healing. And I know they have no idea what it will look like. They simply know to ask.

They ask like the children they no longer are. They ask like the God they believe in told them to. They ask for life without knowing what it will look like. Without knowing if He will reach down and regenerate the cells that have mutinied or if He will wrap her in both arms and whisper, "Enough."

But there they are asking. And my wide eyes are wet because I know He is there too, standing in the thick of that group of pleading women on the maroon steps of a church in Virginia at noon after the Sunday-morning service. I know He is wrapping them up in Himself, absorbing their grief, their pleas, their desperation. I know, because He said so.

"For where two or three are gathered in my name, there am I with them" (Matt. 18:20 NIV).

And my whole hard heart that has been curdled with doubt throughout this morning's service crumbles with the realization. That one way or another—He will heal her. One way or another—He will answer those prayers. I realize that Rema knows that. So do Connie and Janice and Trudy and Karine and Bunni and Christy and Denise.

They pray for His will to be done, trusting that it will be good—whether on earth or in heaven. They pray it together, and together create a fortress of courage and faith for her to rest in. And He is there to help lay the cement and stack the bricks. He is builder and carpenter and healer and good God. He is good. He is good. He is only good.

And the altar they unknowingly build right there, on the steps my kids have so often jumped off when they should know better, testifies to their faith and His goodness—and I will not forget.

I will not quickly forget.

"Jacob built an altar there and called the place God of Bethel because it was there that God had revealed Himself to him when he was fleeing from his brother" (Gen. 35:7).

Because He reveals Himself in the paper-thin moments when our need brushes up against His willingness to answer. And those women, they showed me courage and hope in trusting that His will is what's best. On Sunday mornings and every day of the week.

They showed me that showing up looks like prayer as well as tears. It looks like faith as well as doubt. It looks like believing even when the doctors have given up hope. Because we have a hope that looks nothing like this world, and we have a faith that "is the substance of things hoped for, the evidence of things not seen" (Heb. 11:1 KJV). They showed me what shared grief looks like when it stands shoulder to shoulder. How sharing the grief is what keeps us from being swallowed up by it, being drowned by it.

The world we live in has such contradictory views of grief, doesn't it? On the one hand, it can embarrass us terribly. It can make us feel awkward, and while we might show up for the initial diagnoses, it's hard to keep participating in the grief of our friends over the long run because it's so exhausting. We're good at sadness. We like a good cry. But grief? Grief is its own diagnosis. Grief isn't on anyone else's time line. And grief can make us incredibly uncomfortable around those grieving.

Then on the opposite end of the spectrum is the current culture of grief voyeurism. We have a morbid obsession with grief that isn't actually our own, grief that can't actually touch us with its cold fingers. A grief we can watch from a distance without any threat of it actually choking the life out of us. The kind of grief we experience via blog posts or view on talk shows sandwiched between a sports shoe commercial and a model who wants to convince us that her shampoo will wash away all our gray.

That kind of grief can present a titillating fascination because it's not ultimately about grieving. It's not about carrying someone else's sorrow as if it were our own. Instead, it's about using someone else's sorrow to give us a "good cry," a delicious emotional catharsis at the expense of someone else's devastation.

We get to enjoy that kind of cheap cry therapy without once shouldering any of the actual weight of the grief itself. It downgrades grief to a spectator sport, while being willing to "mourn with those who mourn" requires active participation. It requires getting our hands dirty with the snot and tears of someone else. With their dirty dishes and undone laundry and the eyes of their kids that keep asking for an explanation when no one has a good one to give. To actually sit in that grief beyond the few minutes it takes us to well up while reading a tragic news story is an act of courage.

Do we have it in us, though, to go the distance? Do we have it in us to keep walking with our friends long after the last funeral notes have dissolved, the months of joblessness have settled in, the adoption celebrations have faded, and the nights of attachment disorder have bled into years? Where will we be in those moments? Those moments that aren't emotional highs. Those moments that rattle through us and won't let go and are shackled to the lives of our friends. Will we stay? Will we stay through the long, cold dark with them or will we tire and want to untie ourselves from a story that doesn't have a convenient or happy ending?

Will we be more than what Anna Whiston-Donaldson, who lost her twelve-year-old son in a flash flood, calls "drive-by" friends? Out of the depth of her own pain, her honesty will take your breath away—how she admits that before her own loss, "I'[d] been more of a drive-by friend, the kind who reaches out once or twice and hopes the situation will be resolved quickly. I care. I cry. I pray. But I don't stick around long. I'm the type of friend you would want around for a broken ankle but not for chronic depression. I get a sense I'm learning from the women who show up for me. Who offer themselves up in a way that I've never had the guts to do. They are braver than they think."[3]

I can't get Anna's haunting words out of my head: "Death breaks things, even friendships."[4] Jesus said, "There is no greater love than to lay down one's life for one's friends" (John 15:13 NLT). Perhaps we need to take a closer look at that challenge. Because I think we've diminished its power by limiting it to acts of heroism. Instead, there must be a million daily ways we can lay down our lives in the course of a lifetime. Lay down our own lives and align ourselves with the grief of our friends if we want to have a hope of our friendships surviving grief, friendships that aren't shattered by what we can't share. Anna describes the practical, tangible ways her community did this after their son died—one-line "I love you" text messages, cards in the mail, a neighbor mowing their lawn before his own, people who cooked for them.[5] She describes a web of shared grief that lay down on the cold, cracked ice of their loss and held on to them to prevent them from falling through. The shared grief "redistributed the weight, making a web, or a snowflake pattern that reache[d] to the far edges of the pond and onto solid ground to keep us safe."[6]

When I think of my own life preservers after my mom died, I remember the friends who kept showing up even when they weren't invited. The fact that they were all teenagers amazes me in retrospect. How they were unfazed by the insecurities that haunt adult friendships in the wake of deep grief. Their un-self-consciousness was a gift to me. How they asked me questions about her, about her last days, and they actually wanted to know. They were unembarrassed by the loss that had blown through me and were willing to let me still be me. They'd come by on Sunday afternoons, unannounced, and pick me up for coffee dates. If they'd called beforehand, maybe I would have chosen to stay home and hide.

I still remember the yellow Mini Cooper and the four of us stuffed into its insides, with the windows down and spring blowing through the backseat. They'd laugh and chat, and I'd look out the window. But as long as I was with them I could keep the bits and pieces of myself from blowing away on the breeze that sifted through the car. They anchored me to everyday life when I felt separated from everything by a film of water. Like I was under the heavy ocean looking up at the surface, unable to reach it, unable to breathe, unable to speak. But I could see them there on the other side, and when they picked me up or arrived to visit over cups of tea and South African rusks in the backyard, I was dragged back to the surface and would blink, surprised to find that life was still happening and I was still a part of it.

But one visit, one coffee date, one tender conversation is not enough. Because grief doesn't have a time limit. It doesn't run out at a convenient, fixed date. It loops. It's on an endless loop. We might grow away from it only to find ourselves days and even years later right back at the familiar, terrible place where we started. And will we still have friends willing to go there *again* with us when they'd done their duty by us? Done it above and beyond and don't want to be dragged back to the beginning. Especially when we don't want to either. The difference being that we don't have a choice in the matter and they do.

C. S. Lewis described it like this: "For in grief nothing 'stays put.' One keeps on emerging from a phase, but it always recurs. Round and round. Everything repeats. Am I going in circles, or dare I hope I am on a spiral? But if a spiral, am I going up or down it? How often—will it be for always?—how often will the vast emptiness astonish me like a complete novelty and make me say, 'I never realized my loss till this moment'? The same leg is cut off time after time."[7]

We live in a culture that values deadlines and timeliness. But to "weep with those who weep" is to enter into a process that isn't on a set schedule and can't promise a definite end point. It's simply being willing to be available. Indefinitely. That's a terrible and tall order. I know it. But "shouting stern advice at people through a megaphone from a very great height never did do much good."[8] No, instead, as Adrian Plass writes in his brutally honest letters that unpack both faith and doubt, "the principle of incarnation is pretty much the only way to go when it comes to these encounters. Go down to where they are, tie their shoelaces, make them a sandwich, put an arm round their shoulders and start the climb back together."[9]

It doesn't always have to look like tears. It can look like play dates—simply showing up and watching your friend's kids while she naps or cries or takes a bath. It can look like planning an extra meal a week and delivering it whether she asked for it or not. It can look like sitting on the couch and binge-watching mindless TV for hours together. Just being a buffer between her and her grief, a physical reminder that she is not physically alone with her sorrow. Laying our lives down for our friends can translate into a hundred daily inconveniences that simply remind her without using actual words, "You are not alone."

Laying our lives down for our friends can translate into a hundred daily inconveniences that simply remind her without using actual words, "You are not alone."

Because grief is one of the most deeply isolating and lonely emotions, no one can carry it for you and no one can cure you of it and no one can relate to the exact degree that you're experiencing it. It's a terrible, devouring monster, and without people surrounding you, sitting on the sofa next to you, stopping by to chat about the kids or laugh about a story you'd forgotten, you'll slowly disappear into the sinkhole of grief and coming back out again will take an act of God.

So, that's what He gives us when He gives us friends who aren't afraid or embarrassed by our grief. Or even braver, friends who *are* afraid and embarrassed and who keep showing up anyway. Who don't just say, "Let me know how I can help," but who initiate help themselves. Because grief is exhausting, and having to think of the ways we need to be helped when we're drowning in sinking sand is impossible. So friends who feel awkward but who come over anyway and put in a load of laundry or go pick up groceries or stock the fridge with milk, those friends help stabilize us, help remind us that the ground underneath us might just be safe to walk on again. That thing you thought about doing for your grieving friend, that you thought was "too small" or "too pushy" or "too whatever"—*do it anyway*. Show up. She might not thank you for it. But she will have one more life preserver to hold on to and it will be you. In between your car-pool runs and making dinner, you will have saved a life, inch by seemingly insignificant inch.

Because the act of offering yourself and your faith to a friend who's lost hers is an act of heroism, plain and simple. Thank you. Thank you for being willing to give away parts of yourself to that friend who needs a way to patch herself back together—thank you for being her glue. People are the glue that put other people back together. Or, in the words of my friend Christie Purifoy, "the Light of God in another—that is the glue for all our broken pieces."[10]

The hardest conversation I have ever had was with a friend who'd lost her daughter. A gorgeous eighteen-month-old born under the jacarandas in South Africa just a month before my son was also born into a South African spring. They'd played during church together and done first birthday parties, and steps and splash pools together, and then suddenly one afternoon that gorgeous, sweet, chub of a baby girl with her wispy brown hair was gone in the most violent and devastating way. I was an ocean away back in America when it happened. And I held on to the phone screaming and crying as the news came over the airwaves to my disbelieving ears, and I wanted to hang up; I wanted to make it be not real. And months later when I was home again, I knew that my friend, my fellow mother with the empty crib in her house, would want to make it not real too.

She kept avoiding my calls. She kept rescheduling where and when we'd get together. First we were going to meet in a coffee shop, and then she said maybe it wasn't a good day after all and finally she said I should just stop by her house. I knew I needed to. I knew she needed me to. But it was excruciating. It was painful. I stood in her kitchen anyway as she made tea, and I made myself remember and I made myself tell her all my favorite memories about her daughter. And we laughed. We laughed so hard at some of the funny stories of toddlers, and then we cried and poured tea and stirred in milk and sugar and walked out to the patio under the bougainvillea. We sat together, two moms who'd survived sleepless nights and all the dirty diapers in the world and the shock of new motherhood, and she told me it was so good to talk about her precious tiny human. How she'd dreaded it and how surprised she was that it was so good to remember together.

Being willing to weep with your friends will take courage. It will take deliberate choices. It will sometimes take inviting yourself over even when it feels awkward and like an imposition, because if you keep putting it off, the window will close and you'll have missed the chance to be a living, breathing, weeping form of life support. They need you. Especially when they don't want you.

They might not recognize it at first. It might take years for them to really appreciate from the inside out what you did for them. But they will. There will be a day when a fellow mom or student or colleague wonders out loud to the group how to encourage the teenage daughter of a friend—a mom who's just been diagnosed with cancer. And they'll remember. They'll remember how you loved them, how you encouraged them, with nothing more than your willingness to show up and laugh and cry and sit right there with them, alongside them, in the middle of their most awful moments, and they'll pass that story on.

I remember.

I have these scars, and they won't let me forget. But more significantly, they've opened soft spaces in my heart where the memories spill out and help me wrap my own story around the people I'm trusted with who are now living their own dark and desperate valleys.

Grief and joy are two sides of the same coin—sometimes separated by only a hair's breadth as that coin spins in the balance. So that our tears can turn to laughter in the blink of a soggy minute, and our friends need us to be willing to come and carry their grief and share our joy and remind them how to find themselves again there in the murky dark on an otherwise ordinary Tuesday afternoon.

Be Willing to Share Each Other's Joy

When the cancer lost and Peggy Lopez found her way safely home to Jesus, how could she have known that mere months later a smaller version of her with dark, curly hair and just as brave would stand up in front of all the pews of faces and voluntarily lay down her life?

With head held barely higher than the side of the pool, she told us what a ten-year-old feels when watching a woman after God's own heart prepare to meet Him. How she knew she wanted to follow in Peggy's footsteps and entrust her life to Jesus, so that she might also be raised with Him.

How she stood in the water and looked right out at us who are much older and most of the time think ourselves much wiser. How her voice never shook and how she spoke a truth much older even than Jim and Ginny, sitting there in the center aisle back row, and all their combined lifetime of faithfully following Jesus.

How she and the three Lawson kids before her did what children have always been doing—they came to Jesus. They came as easily as it is difficult for many moms and dads to come. They came running. They came with joy. They came with Bible verses memorized and testimonies that stretched back to when they were three—no memory imprinted into their young minds that didn't hold an echo of the Jesus truth that has been their story since birth.

They may have stood on tippy toes so that they could see over the edge of the baptismal pool, but their faith was rock solid underneath.

So much joy running down, dripping wet right there in the everyday sanctuary where we sang and prayed and where we sat on the steps all those months ago and asked God to heal Peggy Lopez. Asked like the children we no longer are. Asked like the God we believe in told us to. Asked for life without knowing what it would look like. Without knowing if He would reach down and regenerate the cells that had mutinied or if He would wrap her in both arms and whisper, "Enough."

Today we watched the children who watched us ask, lay down their lives in testimony to the Jesus who did heal Peggy. With bare feet and their wet clothes. Leading all the grown-ups behind them.

"Where, O death, is your victory? Where, O death, is your sting?" (1 Cor. 15:55 NIV).

And when Pastor James raised their small, dripping heads up out of the water, little fingers tightly blocking their noses from the water, the whole congregation broke into applause, on our feet with the joy of new life. The joy of watching the living testimony of how Christ has defeated death. How Christ has walked into the dark and offered Himself ransom for all our grief, our fear, our desperate lives unable to produce a single good thing without Him. Tears streaming down my face, I clapped till my palms ached and my heart hurt just as bad with the kind of joy that is an undeserved gift. The kind that stretches you wide open because it's almost impossible to fit it all into one human body.

That Sunday, it was easy to rejoice with those who were rejoicing. To celebrate the faithful lives of little children promising to follow Jesus through their lisps and with eyes wide with wonder. It was the joy of angels and parents, and it was utterly infectious and I wanted to catch every breath of it.

But there are other days.

There are days when someone else's joy feels more like a threat than a celebration. The bizarre underbelly of joy that taints when it should encourage. That threatens when it should inspire. That diminishes when it should enlarge.

Ask any woman struggling with infertility how she feels when she's invited to just one more baby shower. Ask any mom who's lost a child how she feels when his team makes the playoffs, and she has to sit through night after night of not getting to go to basketball practice anymore. Ask any motherless daughter how Mother's Day feels or any aspiring author what it's like to hear your friend's book hit the best seller's list.

There are glorious days where joy comes naturally to us. But there are others when it feels just as heavy a burden to carry as grief. Because celebrating someone else's joy, rejoicing with them, can feel like admitting out loud that thing we don't have, that thing we're desperate for. Being willing to rejoice anyway, being willing to see past your own disappointment and enter into your friend's joy, is the very essence of being willing to lay down your life for your friend. And Jesus has told us that there is no greater love than this.

When celebrating with friends comes easily, thank God and enjoy every moment. But when it comes hard, lean into Jesus and ask Him to lend you His feelings so that you don't miss out on the gift of getting to be the gift to someone else. And for those of us who are rejoicing, let's not forget our friends on the high of our happiness. Let's remember our people who may struggle to throw confetti. Let's give them the gift of both understanding as well as acknowledging their unique season.

Shauna Niequist shares a story of what that looks like. Struggling through excruciating years of infertility and loss, she wrote on her blog how badly she wished she could just smash something, break something, hammer all her raw feelings to bits and pieces with a sledge hammer and a pair of safety goggles. And then a friend who'd just announced her pregnancy invited Shauna to lunch. It could have been terribly awkward—all that joy sitting across the table from all that raw pain. But Shauna describes the surprise moment when her friend handed her a pair of safety goggles and said she'd be willing to smash things in shared pain and solidarity with Shauna any day of the week.[11] Gracious joy making room for shared grief.

In Oswald Chambers' words, "It is impossible to exhaust God's love, and it is impossible to exhaust my love if it flows from the Spirit of God within me."[12] We can always borrow God's feelings of joy when we're struggling to find our own. He promises to pour Himself out into us and then through us, and the only thing we have to do is bring willingness to the equation. We have to be willing to receive His joy and then be willing to pass it on to our friends.

Celebrating with someone else can be an act of spiritual discipline, a choice similar to the decision to willingly enter into her grief. Neither is guaranteed to come easily or naturally. But both are possible if we are willing. Adrian Plass, Christian satirist and fellow perpetual worrier, puts it this way: "The good news . . . is that God can use us whatever our weaknesses and fears, as long as we are willing to be obedient when the time comes for action."[13]

And the time will come. It will come when you least expect it. It will come when it's inconvenient. It will come when you're not prepared. What you do then will be the gift you give your friend. How you respond—with either grief or joy. And don't let the fear of getting it wrong stop you. We all get it wrong. Sometimes more often than we get it right. But Jesus, He is second chances times infinity, and He will never turn down a request for help to try again and He will always show up with you.

On that doorstep, in that minivan with the engine still running as you drop off a meal. Between the words that aren't spoken. He will show up and your friend will see Him in your face, your tears, your laughter. He promised it. In His very own words He told His own friends, "Whatever you did for one of the least of these brothers and sisters of Mine, you did for Me" (Matt. 25:40). He doesn't take days off. He isn't embarrassed by desperate grief or unbridled, indecent joy. He embodied both. Literally. We can trust Him to give us the words. And to fill in all the blank spaces and awkward silences with His own tender presence. Both become a shared experience of a shared God who is the bridge that connects us across the joys and sorrows that He won't let divide us.

LIVE LIKE THE KINGDOM OF GOD IS A CO-OP, NOT A COMPETITION

"Even though I'm a seventy-something grandma, comparison never seems to leave me alone." —Arlys[1]

IT FEELS LIKE SUCH an embarrassing admission—that you often fall down the rabbit hole of comparing yourself to other people. But it can suck you in and suck the life out of you. And it doesn't seem to have any age limit—you're never too young or too old to get sucked into the sinking sand of comparing yourself to someone else. Comparison is always a trap, but we can learn to escape it together.

Of all the insidious ways a friendship can disintegrate, comparison must be one of the worst. Because it cuts at the very heart of what your friends most want to share and celebrate with you or you with them. The thing your friend is the most excited to share will become the thing she wishes she could hide to prevent your jealousy. And jealousy will rob you blind, smash in your self-image, trash your dreams, and tar and feather your best friends before you even realize it's happening.

Comparison will eat at the heart of everything you love the most.

Love to grow a business, build a brand, market your mojo? Comparison will tell you that you should have done it differently, done it like she did, done it years ago to have been successful.

Love to write? Comparison will whisper it's pointless when nobody reads your blog, your journal, your eBook, your fiction anyway. That your stories are lame and who cares what happened to a girl growing up in your neighborhood anyway?

Love to make art? Comparison will tell you that without a degree, a gallery, a show, an Etsy shop, you're a fake. And, that even if you have those things, they'll never live up to the other artists in your circle.

Love to cook? Comparison will tell you that your pots and pans would shame Julia Child and desecrate her recipes.

Love to connect? Comparison will undermine your friendships by making you so desperate for the lives, houses, careers, and opportunities of your friends that you can no longer stand to be around them.

Comparison drives up to take that dream we love, that calling we're following, or that friendship we cherish and wrenches it away from us and grinds it up into dirt and speckled gravel under irreverent tires.

Comparison is exhausting and self-destructive. But a sure antidote to comparison is encouragement. Choosing to encourage instead of compare is a powerful defensive play. But it doesn't always come easy. It is hard, deliberate work. For every single one of us. So let's get to it.

Beware of Comparison Drive-By's

A few years back, I was at a conference standing around chatting with several women—old friends and new. And we got to talking about friendship. About walking the difficult line of cheering for our sisters while secretly coveting their success. Many of the women turned to me and exclaimed how good I am at this encouragement thing. Like it comes naturally. Like maybe it's easier for me. And I was stunned.

If only they could see inside my head. If only they could tune into my internal monologue. If only they knew about my late nights trying to talk myself off the ledge of thinking myself a worthless waste of time because I didn't do it like she did, accomplish it in the same amount of time as they did, or get recognized by that group.

There is a dark thing that hides at the fringes of my faith. I can feel it there. Lurking in the shadows. Waiting.

Waiting for the unkind word from someone I work with, church with, or raise children with.

Waiting for a ninety-degree commute stuck in bumper-to-bumper grid-lock in the ancient car with no air-conditioning.

Waiting for the blog that is prettier, bigger, or more beloved than mine to catch my attention.

Waiting for the mom who is more organized, more disciplined, more engaged than I am.

Waiting for the house that is cleaner, bigger, more HGTV than mine.

Waiting for the job, the opportunity, the invitation that is more glamorous, desirable, interesting than my right now.

And in that moment, I feel it slink out of the shadows and onto my shoulder. Gently it strokes my hair, caresses my neck, and begins to whisper in my ear.

It whispers, "Unfair. Poor you. You *deserve* more."

It understands me. It pets me. It tells me, "You *should* be angry. It's your right to feel frustrated. They don't know how hard you have it."

It offers me the opportunity to rant and sulk and feel justified in doing so. More often than I care to admit, I have allowed the dark thing to cover my mouth with a hard, hot hand and speak petty words on my mute behalf. It is never pretty.

But sometimes, sometimes I remember what a lie sounds like.

I recognize it by how it always puts me at the center of an equation and everyone else in the red. How it leaves out important elements and twists others to suit its own ends. How it refuses to take delight in anything that doesn't belong to me. And on those occasions, I crane my neck around to address the creature squatting on my neck. It does not like that.

"Liar," I say. "Cheat!"

"You are trying to sneaky, sneaky snatch my peace, my contentment, and my friendship away from me. But you cannot tug-of-war me away from my faith. And you do not speak for me."

With each word I gain courage and volume. And with each word the thing deflates before my eyes until I can reach up with one hand and pull it off me.

Free.

And I do what we do with any parasite—I crush it, burn it, flush it. And apply the appropriate ointment:

> Now this is what the LORD says—the One who created you, [daughter], and the One who formed you, [child]—"Do not fear, for I have redeemed you; I have called you by your name; you are *Mine*. . . . Because you are precious in My sight and honored, and I love you, I will give people in exchange for you and nations instead of your life. Do not fear, for I am with you." (Isa. 43:1, 4–5a)

The best way to identify a lie is to compare it to the truth.

And when I begin to see my value through my Savior's eyes, to hear how I am precious in His sight, how He wants to honor me and love me and gather me and my children into His arms, and how He has created us all for His glory, all other comparisons dissolve into irrelevance. And the fringes of my faith grow stronger and better at keeping out the dark.

But it's hard. It's so hard. It's much harder than it looks from the outside. And it's ongoing. It's a battle we fight day in and day out, deadline in and deadline out, conversation in and conversation out.

We live in a world where in totally unexpected seconds, we can stumble into a drive-by comparison shooting when only moments earlier we were filled up with the contentment of our own lives. Just last weekend, I stood at the door of our living room watching my people play across the floor. There were piles of laundry and undone dishes. There were Legos and tiny dolls and all the miniature clothes to go with them. It was a mess, and it filled me up with a kind of sticky, delicious happiness. All these people were mine to call "home," mine to love, mine to do life with in this house tucked behind a row of pine trees.

I was so full of the kind of love that surprises us on the best kind of ordinary days that I couldn't move. I just stood in awe, watching the wonder of my life play out before my eyes. The kind of wonder I never could have explained to my teenage self who was so set on being cool and fitting in. The kind of wonder that comes from seeing enough of the broken parts of life to recognize the moments that are highlighted by the tender light of everyday miracles. I took a photo so that I could remember it and then turned back down the hall to our bedroom, because the ultimate miracle was that my family had sent me to enjoy a Saturday-afternoon nap.

As I climbed into bed, I reached for my phone to set an alarm. But then I made the mistake of opening Instagram. And right before my very eyes I watched my little cocoon of contentment explode into a million pieces of discontent. I scrolled through photo after photo of women who'd been invited to a retreat I didn't even know about, authors who were writing profound words while I had my hair in a dirty ponytail and was still wearing my pajamas. Just like that, I felt the bullets of the comparison drive-by ricochet off my delight and shatter all my satisfaction into miserable, little one-inch-by-one-inch shards of envy. It literally took seconds. One breath I was as fulfilled by my life as I've ever been, and in the next breath I gasped out the miserable grumblings of a toddler who sits surrounded by piles of presents, obsessed over the one thing she didn't get.

Victims of comparison drive-bys litter the Internet, our women's groups, our book clubs, Facebook updates, churches, and circles of friends. We live in a world where there are virtual warehouses of new ways we can find to covet our neighbor's house, family, and life these days. Nothing is as terrifying as thinking you don't matter because you can't do it like she does.

And, this is exactly the lie that Satan wants to feed us and that we, in our sinful skins inherited from Adam and Eve, are so eager to swallow—believing that we need what she has to ensure that we matter. That the lives we've been gifted are somehow diminished by the successes, joys, opportunities, or accomplishments of others. As Priscilla Shirer writes in her book *Fervent*, which unpacks the strategies of effective prayer, "If I were your enemy, I'd devalue your strength and magnify your insecurities until they dominate how you see yourself, disabling and disarming you from fighting back, from being free, from being who God has created you to be. I'd work hard to ensure that you never realize what God has given you so you'll doubt the power of God within you."[2]

One of the best ways to neutralize our effectiveness in the kingdom of God is for us to be tricked into thinking that we don't count. To give up, to sit down, to call it quits, to cry on frustrated winter afternoons that if we can't do it just like she does then it's not worth doing it at all. "He'd rather conspire to keep you in a constant state of mourning, grieving over who you *wish* you were, instead of relishing who you really *are*, exacerbated by insecurity and crippling self-doubt."[3] This is genius marketing on Satan's part. Our natural pull toward sin, combined with his ability to bait us, can convince us that there is only one job, one opportunity, one book, one business model, one design, one podcast, one assignment, one calling that counts. Let's be honest, Satan really doesn't have to work that hard to distract us. One call, one e-mail, one conversation, and the bullets of comparison ricochet through us and everything we thought we believed, leaving us questioning God and His purpose for our lives.

No wonder that this desperate, self-centered desire is at the root of every single other sin. "In fact, Christian philosopher Francis Schaeffer says that every one of the Ten Commandments can be summed up in the last: 'You shall not covet' (Exod. 20:17). He states, 'Anytime that we break one of the other commandments of God, it means that we have already broken this commandment, in coveting.'"[4]

In unpacking what makes some relationships safe and others harmful, Drs. Cloud and Townsend underline in their book *Safe People* the terrible, destructive power of what comparison breeds—coveting and envy. "Envy makes us resent people who have something we don't have. It feeds on itself and is ultimately self-destructive. When we envy, the very people who are loving, safe, and generous become the bad guys in our eyes."[5]

That sounds extreme, doesn't it? That sounds a million miles away from our ordinary Thursday lives where we know how to be polite and how to congratulate people and often don't recognize the quiet resentment building in our souls toward other people. We go about our business and our car pool and our classes and it becomes almost an unconscious decision to avoid their calls, ignore their messages, scroll past their Facebook statuses without leaving a comment.

That's the noose of comparison and envy tightening around your neck without you even realizing it. That's the dark thing on your shoulder sliding its awful fingers around your throat till it's hard to swallow past that lump of dissatisfaction that grows bigger and bigger every time you think about that friend and how "unfair" it is that she has what you want. We might be shocked if someone actually read our thoughts out loud. Because we're so good at pretending we're not really thinking them, not really feeling all that terrible anger toward the person who has what we think should be ours.

Because in Satan's kingdom we are tempted by our envy—our discontentment—to "hate other people for having what we want. Envy says, 'What is inside me is bad. What is outside me is good. I hate anyone who has something I desire.'"[6] This kind of hate is why Cain killed Abel (Gen. 4), who got the recognition for a sacrifice that Cain thought he deserved, why Saul plotted against David (1 Sam. 18–19) when the crowds went wild for David's exploits that far outstripped Saul's own; why Rachel resented Leah (Gen. 30:1–22) for the children she so easily conceived; and why they both dragged their servant girls into their bitter feuding over who had more kids, more affection, more status. This ugly weed of hatred grows out of the seed of jealousy and chokes the life out of the hater as much as out of the person it hates.

And so without a single confrontation, without raised voices or even a conscious acknowledgment of what's happening, a friendship can be decimated by the simple buildup of a toxic and insurmountable wall of jealousy. So that every time our friend tries to reach out or connect, she smacks into the invisible wall we've built between her success and our jealousy. After a while, she stops trying. And then we get to be angry with her all over again for abandoning us.

The cycle is vicious and viciously effective. And it relies on another lie—the myth of scarcity. Because in Satan's kingdom, where we each want to be our own gods, there is no room for sharing, there is never enough to go around, and everything must be grabbed and hoarded to make sure we survive. But God's Kingdom is about abundance, about multiplying, about giving with shocking generosity and still having leftovers. It's about taking the tiny offerings that our insecure hearts are willing to trust to Jesus and watching as He prays, thanks His Father, and then feeds everyone around us, including ourselves, with those small loaves and fishes. His Kingdom breaks and breaks and breaks our own expectations, always multiplying, always offering more, always blessing, in astonishing, unexpected, jaw-dropping ways.

Satan "wants you lifeless, disengaged, brainwashed into believing you have nothing to offer."[7] But the carpenter and friend of fishermen, who called a motley crew to follow Him and calls you and me each by name, wants all of you, every single breathing bit, to live its fullest, deepest, truest self in His Kingdom. And to do that, He will deliberately break us open so that He can multiply all that we have available, all that we can bring to the Kingdom table to feed the people around us. He's not trying to take something away from us; His intention is to multiply what He's already given us. All that DNA that God has packed with potential and promise, He wants to see shared and spread. It's the ancient promise first spoken to Abram and then passed down through His children all the way to the Messiah and on to each of us, "I will bless you, I will make your name great, and *you will be a blessing*" (Gen. 12:2, emphasis mine).

Any blessing that shows up in our lives—from the breath that expands our lungs, the blood that runs through our veins, the children who wail in our living rooms, the work that waits at the end of long commutes, or the people who gather around our dining room tables and call us friends—every single one of these is a living picture of God's generosity to us. Given to bless us. And intended to bless others. Blessings are not for hoarding, they're for forwarding. Because that is how we reflect God's glory back to Him. "We are the public manifestation of God's glory. When the Earth [and its inhabitants] reflects His holiness, we call it glory."[8]

Because if we were to look up, look away from what we wish we had, if we would pay attention to right where we are, where God has purposefully, tenderly placed us, we might see that in order to have rubbernecked so hard and so far to the left and right, we've been standing with stubborn heels ground down on top of the hand-painted, one-of-a-kind life art crafted just for us.

We are each of us unique. A fingerprint swirl of utterly and totally incomparable. We were designed with ineffable tenderness and deliberate purpose: "Before I formed you in the womb *I knew you*, before you were born *I set you apart*; I appointed you as a prophet to the nations" (Jer. 1:5 NIV, emphasis mine). These words aren't cliché or trite or precious sentiments intended only for baby birth announcements. These words are the promise from a God to His child. A promise from a God who always lives up to His word. So hear these words with fresh ears:

Before you were born, you were already known and seen and set apart for specific, profound purposes. So there is no way that your girlfriend or favorite pastor's wife or neighbor or office mate could possibly steal that thing you were built to do. You don't need to panic or hoard or hide. You only need to answer. Just say, yes. Say with preteen Samuel the simple, obvious words, "Speak, for Your servant is listening" (1 Sam. 3:10). Let's listen to Jesus' promises over us and stop tuning into the lie that there won't be anything left over for us once everyone else has had their slice of the pie.

Seven years ago, I was commuting into work to a job that was a terrible fit, driving hours each way with daycare drop-offs that made me think amputating a limb might have been easier and more appealing. I was stuck in traffic. I was listening to endlessly overplayed songs on our Christian radio station. I was discovering a desperation to write my own stories that I didn't know I'd had, and I was anxiously waiting for the time to live out this new passion.

I didn't know how it would look. I just knew it wasn't what I was doing every day from nine to five. And I'd spin spirals of crazy questions in my head, "What happens if I'm stuck in this circle of sameness? What happens if I get too old for something new? What happens if someone else gets there first?"

On the days I didn't drive to work, I took the train. And then I walked with hundreds of other morning commuters over the knobby streets of downtown Washington, DC. I walked and tried to make sense of it all. All these years in a skin that didn't seem to fit. Around me, friends were signing book deals, launching conferences. Inside me, I had this hunger to cheer for all the women who knew what it felt like to walk in these uncomfortable shoes. But instead, I tried to make it home in time for the last pickup at preschool. And while I worried my way home through gridlock, these questions would play on a loop in my head, "What if this is my life? What if there isn't anything else? What if my dreams have nowhere to go? What if I'm too old and too many other people are already in line ahead of me?"

There was a day I arrived at work that is printed on my mind as clearly as a photocopy. I remember how the doorknob looked. It was a kind of tarnished bronze set into a white door in a DC row house. It always stuck, and my key was uselessly stubborn to turn. I stood there trying to turn that handle on a door that led into a building where I didn't want to be at a job I didn't feel called to, and I couldn't get it to open.

My hand was on the handle, and I can remember exactly the clear thought that dropped into my mind.

There's enough work in the Kingdom for everyone.

I stood, doorknob in hand, and let those words just sink in all the way down to my toes.

There's enough work in the Kingdom for *everyone.*

What she's doing, what they're hosting, what your Instagram and Facebook friends are experiencing—that's their piece of the Kingdom. That's their plot of land, and they're supposed to be working at it faithfully. But you? You have your own spot in the Kingdom garden. You have your own soil waiting for seeds and seasons and harvest.

And then I was inside and up three flights of stairs at my desk.

There's enough work in the Kingdom for everyone.

I kept commuting for large chunks of my day and writing for large chunks of my night. And as slowly and delightfully as a chia pet that finally starts to sprout just when you've given up checking on it, God gave me new tools, different opportunities, and my piece of Kingdom garden caught a vision and some rain. *Because* of where I'd been, what I'd despaired, how I'd wrestled. I needed that job and commute and discomfort. I didn't want them. But I'd needed them.

No one can steal your dream because God has built it into you.

No one can write your book or design your art.

No one can launch your venture like you can.

No one can do that secret impossible that you've got your heart set on the way you can. Because *you* are the DNA of the dream. The Holy Spirit is *in* you. Even if you and a friend both started with the exact same premise, you'd end up glorious worlds apart as distinct as your fingerprints. Because you are.

What God gives you He gives you on purpose. This season is not an accident. You haven't missed the boat. You aren't in a maze. You are just limited by your ability to see. "Faith makes us sure of what we hope for and gives us proof of what we cannot see" (Heb. 11:1 CEV).

But the God who planted that dream? He isn't limited by sight. "And I am certain that God, who began the good work within you, will continue his work until it is finally finished on the day when Christ Jesus returns" (Phil. 1:6 NLT). I am. I am certain of it.

But in the meantime, we have to get up on Mondays and get into our cars and take care of our responsibilities and change the laundry from the washer to the dryer and show up for parent-teacher conferences and work evaluations and figure out how to live without wishing we were living like she does. On those days, here are three things to keep in mind:

1. Be Careful If and How You Confess Your Jealousy

One of the downsides of confession is that while it might make you feel better, it can make your friend feel like she was mauled by a lion she had no idea was stalking her. Author and satirist Adrian Plass describes it like this: "If someone marches up to me and 'confesses' that they've hated me, how does that help me? . . . They walk away, pleased to have got their stuff off their chest, and I'm left reeling."[9]

Growing up Christian, we're taught to confess our sins. And while it is sometimes healthy to confess our sins to the person we've wronged, sometimes it's a case of making ourselves feel better at the expense of making our friends feel worse. This seems to me especially true in the case of jealousy. Confessing jealousy to the person you're jealous of leaves them in a very uncomfortable spot because there's nothing they can do about it. Except maybe start to feel bad and horribly self-conscious of themselves. They can't unmake their gifts and opportunities, and we shouldn't expect them to. They've been content-edly plowing and sowing and tending their row in the Kingdom garden, but after your confession, they may look back over their shoulder and start to feel guilty. Guilty about all those juicy tomatoes that have grown or that crop of potatoes that sprouted with such enthusiasm.

Telling them how jealous you are of their harvest could sow a seed of doubt and regret into a once-joyful gardener's bit of dirt. Confessing your jealousy puts the burden on them instead of where it should be—on you. It unfairly shifts the responsibility to process jealousy in a healthy way from the person in the know to the person who has no clue what's been going on.

If we want to bring jealousy out into the light so that the dark creature eating up our hearts can't continue to whisper its viscous, strangling lies to us anymore, what we need is a safe friend who can be a safe vault for all those dark feelings. Confession can be the key to unlocking that dark room we pre-tend doesn't exist. But let's makes sure that we process the lie that says, "I don't matter if I don't have what she has" with someone who can't be hurt by that confession. That's a brave and hard conversation to have. But it's the prison break Satan hates—it's the way to bash down the walls of comparison and let the Son of God stream bright, sanitizing light into every nook and cranny of envy and jealousy and comparison so that He can burn it all away and make room for fresh growth in our own soil.

That kind of holy, hard conversation doesn't take the friend you've been jealous of hostage. Instead, that kind of conversation with a neutral third party can set you free. There's nothing more liberating than bringing your darkest thoughts out into the light with someone you can trust to speak deep truth into all the hollows that the lie of jealousy has dug into your heart. You might be stunned by what deep relief you get simply from admitting your jealousy and letting someone else sift through it with you, exposing the lies hidden inside it.

This kind of confession to a third party helps keep your initial friendship untainted. It gives your friend a gift she'll never even know about—the gift of continuing to walk confidently in her calling without doubting herself. And without being afraid of how it will impact her friendship with you. In that way, you become the blessing to her as well as a wall of protection around her—guarding her plot in the Kingdom from the enemy who would love nothing more than to sow doubt and insecurity into what she's been asked to grow for the family of God.

One note, though, about the difference between painful confession and preemptive defense. The first can wound a friendship, while the second is one of the best ways I know to protect it.

Once jealousy has started to rot away the supporting beams of a friendship, we need confession; we need to recruit a friend to come in like a trusted contractor and help us repair the damage so that it's safe to walk around in our friendships again. Sometimes, however, that kind of deep, jealousy wood rot hasn't begun yet. Instead, you've just noticed a tiny spot of what might be water damage. And now's the time to intervene. Immediately. Before there's a chance for any of that water to actually stain or strip or rot through the foundation of a friendship.

I've been deeply grateful to the friends who've been brave enough to give me this gift. The friends who've shot me a quick e-mail or phone call as the first drops of jealousy or insecurity have crept into their hearts. And before those thoughts have had even the slightest chance of taking root or causing damage, they've aired them out immediately. They've shone a bright light on them by giving me a quick heads-up that this was something they didn't want to become an issue between us.

And in that moment, because we're taking proactive steps to cut off comparison and stop jealousy before it even gets a chance to start, our friendships have grown deeper and safer. When a friend feels safe enough to share that she sees a speck of potential comparison or insecurity on the horizon, we can both speak truth into each other, reassure each other of our love and trust, and reaffirm all the things we see the other one called to do in the kingdom of God. Then Satan is silenced, and the Holy Spirit scores a powerful preemptive defensive strike.

2. Guard Your Friends from Jealousy

When one of my kids gets what's supposed to be a special one-on-one treat, they can't seem to restrain themselves from rushing into the house when they get home and announcing what they got to everyone else who was left behind. No matter how I prep them, no matter how I tell them it's unkind to brag about our blessings, they still hurtle into that house and bust a frenzied, delighted gut-sharing of the giddy list of all the things that their siblings missed out on. It makes me crazy.

But for us grown-ups who should know better, we're sometimes just as reckless with our blessings as my five-year-old. It's one thing to take delight in God's good gifts; it's another thing entirely to paint them in Technicolor and list them in excruciating detail for everyone around us. Joseph learned the hard way what kind of effect that had on the people around him. We would do well to learn from his experience (Gen. 37).

There is a time to share our opportunities, accomplishments, and joys. But there's also a time to treasure them in our hearts, content with private delight. This is becoming harder and harder in a culture that glorifies sharing every tiny detail of our lives. But we can do better. We can remember to guard the hearts of our friends and find tender ways to share news that we know might cause damage to a friend who we love. Surely the friendship is more significant than the news we're dying to share. Let's keep living Christ's challenge to die to ourselves, even in our moments of deepest accomplishment and grandest success. Let's die to the temptation to flash our news around like giddy children who don't know any better.

Let's constantly be on the lookout for ways to guard our friendships. And sometimes that starts with what comes out of our own mouths or Instagram streams.

We do know better. And if we love our friends deeply, then we'll be deeply concerned with their well-being, and we'll handle our news and their hearts with extra care and consideration. Let's constantly be on the lookout for ways to guard our friendships. And sometimes that starts with what comes out of our own mouths or Instagram streams. Let's take the extra time and care when we're sharing news that we know has the potential to sow comparison and jealousy into a friendship that we hold dear. Let's care more about our friends than our own accomplishments. Let's tread carefully when treading on what we know are the hopes and dreams of the people we hold most dear.

3. Dare to Encourage Instead of Compare

If anyone says, "I love God," yet hates his brother, he is a liar. For the person who does not love his brother he has seen cannot love the God he has not seen. (1 John 4:20)

Some people are so generous with their encouragement, it never fails to surprise in all the best possible ways. They dole it out like piñata candy—it's so wonderful and unexpected every time it falls on your head. My friend Ann will send me voice messages while she's doing her hair or cleaning her kitchen. Whether they're five minutes or fifteen, I can always count on them to be absolutely packed with all the passion and life-giving protein of encouragement. She never runs out, never stops finding new ways to admire my work, my mothering, even my new kitchen countertops or the way I did Zoe's hair this morning. She is generosity set on a delicious, life-giving loop, and it strengthens my bones.

Jessica does the same with her handwritten notes and cards. When I least expect it, for no other reason than that she is my friend, a postcard or box of brownies will arrive in the mail sent as a reminder of her love and friendship, and it never, ever stops being surprising or radically rejuvenating.

They've convinced me that this is a mountain worth dying on—that Christ's Kingdom is always intended to be a co-op and never a competition. After my own battles with comparison, I'm almost fanatical about my insistence that the best antidote to jealousy is choosing instead to encourage. Because it's the only thing I've found that solidly works. The moment I start to feel that sinking feeling of dissatisfaction welling up in me, I know I need to message a friend, give her a call, or post a note telling her what I love about what she's doing. I need to deliberately write down all the ways she's running confidently in her lane that inspire me. Because the more I focus on how her work blesses, the less I'm able to want it for myself. It's hard to hate something that inspires you.

There is power in speaking words of blessing and encouragement over someone else. Proverbs says, "The power of the tongue is life and death—those who love to talk will eat what it produces" (18:21 ISV). A vivid picture—the words we speak will either be the hearty, healthy food that satisfies or the empty junk food that leaves us feeling bloated and dissatisfied.

The best antidote to jealousy is choosing instead to encourage.

Start small and watch it snowball. List the one thing you love most about your friend. Then write down the ways her opportunity or new job or new baby or new book or raise or song or redone living room adds blessing to your own life. Do they offer you hospitality or a safe place for your small group to meet? Do they offer you a chance to hold a tiny package of fresh life in your arms that reminds you Jesus is in the business of making all things new? Or do they offer words to read or listen to or pass on that pour life into your tired ears? Now, go find your friend. E-mail or call or meet for coffee and let her know. Let her know the specific ways that this unique moment in time in her life is a blessing to you. Bless her back with your words and your encouragement. Say the words even if you don't feel the feelings yet.

Speaking all the ways that your friend encourages you through her one-of-a-kind way of living out the purpose God's put on her life will fill up your hungry spaces with the satisfaction of truth instead of the bitter crusts of comparison.

STOP TRYING TO FIND A SEAT AT THE MORE POPULAR TABLE

"I wish I could say I don't feel this way, that somehow I've conquered this desire to be a part of 'the' group—whoever 'the' group is. But alas, I still possess the X-Chromosome so this is as ever constant for me as it is for any woman." —Kelli[1]

NO MATTER HOW OLD we are, I think there's always going to be a teenage girl living inside of us, desperate to be one of the "cool kids." Define *cool* however you like, but inevitably we can trace dissatisfied friendships to this search for the elusive "in" and dissatisfaction with where we find ourselves currently: a perceived "out."

The thing we don't realize in high school, and sometimes we still haven't learned during the minivan-driving years, is that everyone is on the outside of something. But that is only half the story. We are all, each one of us, also on the inside of something—often without even realizing it.

So what we need to learn is that we can either fight to find a way in, or we can love on the women right where we already are. We can obsess over who didn't talk to us or we can focus on the woman right in front of us. We can keep looking for a seat at a more popular table or we can pass the breadbasket and an introduction to the women sitting right beside us.

Everyone is on the outside of something. But that is only half the story. We are all, each one of us, also on the inside of something—often without even realizing it.

It's the story of how asking someone to save you a seat at their table, only to bypass them because you've spotted a seat at a more popular table, can hurt you both.

We can obsess over who didn't talk to us or we can focus on the woman right in front of us.

It's about looking that teenager inside you deep, deep in the eyes, and cupping hands gently around her tender, confused face, and pointing her in the direction of all the IN that's waiting for her. All the ways she's wanted. All the ways she belongs—if she can stop obsessing over her own wants and start focusing on loving the people around her. Letting people inside her invisible walls. And discovering she's been known and seen by the God who names her beloved all along.

There Are No Cool Kids

A few years ago, I was at a church event that included a big sit-down dinner in the sanctuary. Seating at those kinds of events can be so awkward—that whole shuffle of who to sit with and whether you're supposed to save a seat for someone and how you can maneuver yourself into a chair that's actually facing the stage. Or do you need to make your peace with sitting with your back to the speaker all night because that's the seat that you ended up in front of after what often feels like a grown-up game of musical chairs.

Because maybe you stopped to chat in front of the chair on that side of the circle, the one with the table leg situated in such a way that you couldn't properly pull your seat in, and it also happens to be with the back to the stage. Now you're stuck with it, and you'll either be craning your neck around all night or repositioning your chair during the worship, trying not to hit someone in the ankle while at the same time getting yourself turned around in time before the music stops.

So, yeah, these moments are full of all kinds of awkward booby traps.

My friend Nicole is really great at navigating that table shuffle because she's deeply mindful of others and so good at the art of making sure folks are included and comfortably seated. She's a great one to end up next to. Earlier that afternoon, she'd told me that a mutual friend was feeling a bit nervous about being the new girl at the event and had asked Nicole several times to please, please save her a seat. Nicole had repeatedly assured her that she would. And, of course, because she's Nicole, she did.

But when this woman—the woman Nicole saved a space for, the woman she'd been intentionally planning to look out for—walked into the room and Nicole waved her over to the seat she'd saved as promised, something unexpected happened. Halfway toward Nicole, that woman swerved at the last minute to the table just in front of Nicole where several of the event speakers were seated. And right in front of Nicole's surprised eyes, the woman who had counted on Nicole to help her feel included ditched my friend so that she could land a prime spot in between two women more well known.

When Nicole told me the story over coffee, she flung her arms above her head in stunned surprise, and I honestly didn't know what to say. Why do we do that to each other? Ditch the friends we know we can count on for other people who make us feel more important?

But we do, don't we?

C. S. Lewis called it "the quest of the Inner Ring"[2]—this terrible illusion that there's an inner circle we've been left out of coupled with the lie that we've been left out on purpose.

We're built for friendship, yes. We have community in our bones. And when we're desperate and blinded by the taunting mirage of the inner circle, we will drink the sand—angry, gritty, bitter, and confused. And we're not the first. Jesus' closest friends suffered from the very same sickness—this fear of being left out or missing out—that turned them into greedy status hoarders.

Then James and John, the sons of Zebedee, approached Him and said, "Teacher, we want You to do something for us if we ask You."

"What do you want Me to do for you?" He asked them.

They answered Him, "Allow us to sit at Your right and at Your left in Your glory."

But Jesus said to them, "You don't know what you're asking."

. . . When the other 10 disciples heard this, they began to be indignant with James and John." (Mark 10:35–41)

In other words, the other ten were flat-out furious. How dare two brothers try and shoulder everyone else out of the way for the prime real estate at Jesus' side? We do it too; jockeying for position, for the best seat at the best table. It's the kind of prestige grab we are often too subtle, or too polite or too passive-aggressive to say out loud. But Jesus hears it nonetheless.

For me, it can sound like, "Please, Jesus, choose me for that writing assignment, send me to that speaking opportunity, give me that chance to step into the spotlight, light me up with invitations like You've done for her. Set me up on a throne or a headline." It boils down to the same thing, doesn't it? But Jesus patiently teaches me over and over again how gross that greedy spirit is:

Jesus called them over and said to them, "You know that those who are regarded as rulers of the Gentiles dominate them, and their men of high positions exercise power over them. But it must not be like that among you. On the contrary, whoever wants to become great among you must be your servant, and whoever wants to be first among you must be a slave to all. For even the Son of Man did not come to be served, but to serve and to give His life—a ransom for many." (Mark 10:42–45)

And in one paragraph, He deflates my inbred hunger for self-promotion and public attention. He pops the little idol of my own making and instead offers a model of service and sacrifice.

We can be so short-sighted when it comes to friendship. Forgetting that the math of friendship means that more equals less and less equals more. Friendship is always quality over quantity. It's always better when it's slower, fewer, deeper. Friendship is not a race. No one is keeping score. It's not an episode of *Hoarders*. It's not a chance to improve our platform or reputation or status or any of that other nonsense. None of that matters on the days when you're sick in bed, you've lost your voice, and just need a friend. A friend who will show up with soup and offer to take your kids off your hands when there's absolutely nothing in it for her.

That kind of friendship doesn't come from table-hopping. That kind of friendship grows slowly through the everyday moments of doing life alongside each other, living each other's messes, and being comfortable with each other's kids and weird quirks and stories and fondness for eating ice cream right out of the tub. It's the friendship that isn't interested in accolades or titles, but in back porches and honest conversations. These are not small-talk friendships. They are built on service, not status. Again, C. S. Lewis puts it so beautifully into words, how friendships like this bleed into a sense of belonging that can never be manufactured simply by surfing the room for the person who seems the most popular:

> And if in your spare time you consort simply with the people you like, you will again find that you have come unawares to a real inside: that you are indeed snug and safe at the center of something which, seen from without, would look exactly like an Inner Ring. But the difference is that its secrecy is accidental, and its exclusiveness a by-product, and no one was led thither by the lure of the esoteric: for it is only four or five people who like one another meeting to do things that they like. This is friendship. Aristotle placed it among the virtues. It causes perhaps half of all the happiness in the world, and no Inner Ring can ever have it.[3]

Sometimes what looks like an "inner ring" or a clique or an exclusive community might just be the ordinary work of faithful friendship. Let's give those friends the benefit of the doubt and instead of resenting them, let them inspire us to open our eyes to the women who show up repeatedly in our own everyday lives.

Feed the People at Your Table

The thing about having a chance to attend a conference is the sleeping in. The speakers are great. So is the learning and the company. But often what I'm really in it for is the sleeping in. The long, uninterrupted hours of dark bliss when no one comes to me with their nightmares and no one expects me to get up in the middle of the night to take them potty. What can I say, I'm also a sucker for a massive bed that I don't have to share.

But because I love me some sleep, I tend to keep hitting snooze when I'm at a conference. I often come down to breakfast right as it's wrapping up and the breakfast buffet is only offering a few stray strips of bacon and a pancake or two. That's okay by me. Because I didn't have to cook any of it, I'm usually happy with whatever is left over.

However, being late also means that there isn't always someone familiar to sit with. The tables with the people I recognize all have full chairs occupied by people who don't mind getting up on time. I specifically recall this happening one morning in upstate New York. I couldn't spot an empty space next to a single familiar face and got that nervous feeling. And for a ridiculous minute was tempted to take my plate back to my room. But then I caught the eye of a smiling woman at a table with a single empty spot so I took a deep breath. I quit looking over my shoulder to discover if a space had opened up at my friends' table and instead buttered my bagel and made eye contact with the woman next to me and asked her that sacred of all mother questions—"Did you also love the uninterrupted sleep last night?" And I discovered all over again what I should have known all along. Women are deeply welcoming, and over coffee and sausages, there are a hundred different things we can discover we have in common.

And sometimes that's all it takes. Being willing to be present. Asking ordinary questions that uncover how we're all so much alike, and it's like remembering we all speak English to stumble into common conversations about decades of being sleep deprived, the joy of the hot-cooked meal you didn't have to cook yourself, and the itch of a dream you don't know how to put into words but are so relieved someone wants to talk to you about.

Women are hungry for those conversations. We're hungry to be seen and to connect over totally ordinary moments of spilled coffee and that workshop or book or question about faith you need to unpack with someone else. When we're so focused on finding a better seat, a cooler table, a better connection, we're going to miss out on actual community. If that's our focus, then location doesn't matter. It's about connection. It's about having something to actually offer the people sitting at our table. Instead of trying to feed ourselves something else at a better, bigger, shinier table.

What will we feed the hungry women who pull up chairs to our blog table, kitchen table, church table, online book club table, Tuesday-night table? Forget the hundreds you wish would come, the cool or the trending you want to impress; feed the hungry who are already there. Feed them your best. Lay out your story and your life and your generous love for them. Perhaps our friendships are only as big and deep as our hospitality. Because promotions can be lonely and spotlights too bright, but no one ever felt unwelcome in that overstuffed armchair pulled up by the fire, with feet up on the coffee table, and a good friend telling you it's okay to be you.

Perhaps less is more when it comes to practicing friendship. Especially if it gives you time to respond, to encourage, to enjoy the company and conversation for what they really are—people with stories as thick and dog-eared as your own. One on one, we don't need to shout. And that seat you saved is full of a unique individual worth all your undivided attention. Let's show up to the tables where we've been invited. Let's be utterly present and aware of what a gift it is to have people who want to call us their friends.

I don't want to make the mistake of ignoring the people right in front of me, the people who sometimes show up like neighbor kids with their Nerf guns at inconvenient times and my job is simply to open the front door. I can do this. I'm the only one who can do this because this is my house and my yard and I've been given this little plot in God's Kingdom and it's my job to be a good and generous host here. Forget about conferences and stages. If I can't pull out a welcoming chair at my very own dining room table, what business do I have opening a Bible or a book or a message anywhere else?

I'm not always that good at making this obvious connection. I get irritated and tired, and I like my own personal space. Admittedly, there are days I want to be wanted by important people with important titles more than I want to open my fridge to visitors who know me by name and have seen me in my Saturday-afternoon sweatpants. But while I may have those thoughts, I don't want them to be the boss of me.

I want my dining room table to be the boss of me when I'm tempted to set my sights on something "better" than my right-now, right-here friends and neighbors. That table with the big, wide, country planks that have crumbs filling up the cracks. That table with the squeaky chairs we constantly have to repair. That table that can seat stray college students and Tuesday-night friends. That table that is doing its best work when it's messy and has sticky streaks and an extra bench added down one side. That table and my front door are teaching me that the one seat I need to focus on is the one next to me. Not the one across the room or the aisle or even the other end of the table. It's the seat right next to me right now that is supposed to be my teacher. Whether my best friend, a new friend, a relative, a stranger, or one of my own children is sitting in it. Dear God, please help me not to miss the beauty of the seat right next to me.

GIVE THE GIFT OF THE BENEFIT OF THE DOUBT

"I've been preaching to myself. Believe the best, believe the best, believe the best." —Amy[1]

OFTEN A WOMAN'S WORST friend is the voice inside her own head. We are our harshest critics and most unkind friends. And we start to believe that the lies we tell ourselves are what other women are saying about us too. We believe it so hard that we have a tendency to barricade ourselves away from the world and shut down our hearts because we're too afraid to let anyone else into our sacred spaces.

Come along with me as we talk about how we women have mastered the fine and terrible art of having entire extended, multi-part arguments with friends that take place only inside our own heads. But these shadow-boxing matches leave real bruises because they affect how we act around those friends the next time we're sharing air on the actual time-space continuum.

Especially if there's been a whiff of disagreement or misunderstanding that is real, we can easily blow it out of proportion in our own minds. Like a dog with a bone, it's so hard to drop a perceived conflict, analyzing it from every angle and reading dissatisfaction, discontent, and drama into every nuance.

Sometimes there's an actual conflict brewing, but sometimes we're the ones stirring it up by our overreaction to a perceived slight.

Instead of bursting into a conversation with both guns blazing, sometimes simply giving a friend the benefit of the doubt is a powerful way to defuse the situation. It takes courage and a ton of self-control to assume a friend is thinking and talking the best about us instead of presuming she needs to be confronted.

But that's the whole moral of this story: when in doubt, believe the best about your friends.

Just Because You Think It, Doesn't Make It True

I was woken up at 4:45 yesterday morning by my middle child announcing to the darkened room that he'd had a bad dream. About Bigfoot. This particular scary dream is a recurring one in our house, fueled by the fact that during the daylight hours my kids are obsessed with the notion that Bigfoot roams the woods and back brush around our property. They hunt him and watch documentaries about him and read books about him and make their own home movies documenting what they think are his footprints and then are surprised that every now and again they dream about him. And those dreams scare them out of their beds and down the hall into mine and Peter's.

When in doubt, believe the best about your friends.

Now, while I love my kids, I'm not a fan of sharing our sleeping quarters with them. Especially now that they've grown big and gangly with long legs that have a tendency to stretch diagonally across the bed and rudely jab me or their dad in the side as they worm their way into the most comfortable sleeping position on the mattress.

So it was 4:45 a.m. and Micah stood in my doorway and then crawled his way between Pete and me. After we'd all then taken the opportunity to go to the bathroom, have a sip of water, and add an extra blanket to the bed, I found I couldn't fall back asleep. In that predawn window of skies that are still dark and a subconscious that is sleepily awake, I wandered into the dangerous territory some of you might also find familiar. That place between sleeping and waking when our thoughts spiral in on themselves and we replay all the worst conversations and hardest misunderstandings of the last few days, weeks, months. My brain doesn't seem to be consistent when it comes to time lines. It simply picks the most painful things that have happened to me and then puts them on a continuous loop in my head. It's as awesome as it sounds.

So there I was at nearly 5:00 a.m., lying in bed with gritted teeth and racing heart, letting that terrible sense of having been wronged just well up in me and sweep through my body, as hot as the blood in my veins. My friend Janice calls it spiritual torture. How Satan will poke you and prod you with ugly thoughts that are out of context. And how he builds the whole grotesque caricature out of a small kernel of truth. Then he'll march that horrible collection of past hurts and warped memories across your mind at 5:00 a.m. like the Grim Reaper's idea of counting sheep, and you won't be able to sleep as your heart starts to race and your sense of injustice boils over.

This is a real thing. I struggle with it pretty frequently. And in the past I've just laid there, passively, for hours letting the ugliness spawn anger and frustration and a deep sense of self-righteous longing to argue my case, prove myself right, and get in the last stinging word. I used to just let it happen to me. I used to lie immobile on my bed and let the dread spread through me from head to heart to feet. I used to believe that I was a passive victim and that my thoughts were true and that I was entitled to the feelings that came with them.

But at 5:00 a.m. yesterday morning, I knew that was a lie.

I couldn't quite verbalize it, but I knew in the back of my mind, in the thoughts that were still good and whole, that what was happening wasn't something I just had to lie back and take. Because I'm sick of it. I'm sick of the spirals of ick that I can recycle hour after painful hour, and I'm sick of how I feel when I finally stagger out of bed and try to face the day. I'm sick of what it makes me think and especially how it makes me act toward others. How it fills me up with doubt and distrust and how all those feelings linger like a bad taste anytime I try to enter back into conversation with the people who were featured in my 5:00 a.m. horror show.

It is torture. Deep, dark spiritual tortur, and here's the thing—we do not have to let it happen to us. We are not helpless. But that's hard to remember at 5:00 a.m. when the house feels murky and your head feels battered. So I did the one thing I knew I could do—I got out of bed. I simply stood up and walked out of the room and off the nauseating merry-go-round of angry thoughts that were battering me in the dark. I walked into the living room and sat down on the floor and felt the solid truth of the wooden planks beneath me, the chill in the air, and the softness of the blanket I wrapped around me. Real things. Real moments. Tangible atoms instead of frightening bad dreams.

Then I opened my phone and messaged three friends. Not the friends from my bad stream of subconsciousness. That wouldn't have been fair to them. Different friends—friends I trust to always tell me the truth more than I trust myself. I spoke out loud every single thought I was having, and as I spoke them into the air, I watched them dissipate and evaporate in front of my eyes like fog in the light of day. I named the ugly thing, and in naming it, I could confront it: and in confronting it, I watched it disappear.

We forget how, as spiritual creatures grounded in human bodies, our spirits are so deeply affected by the experiences of our bodies.[2] Bodies trapped under blankets in a dark room haunted by terrible thoughts experience all the terrors of a toddler trapped in a bad dream. But sitting up, putting one foot in front of the other, and moving our physical selves away from the place of our spiritual torture can be as radical as a jailbreak. When our bodies shift and adjust to the air of another room, the altered temperature and lighting, then our eyes and cells make adjustments too. And we are distracted away from the thoughts that have been attacking us and can start to plan a counterattack.

Yes, when you're battered by terrible, hate-filled doubts and insecurities at four in the morning, we need to teach ourselves that those thoughts can't be trusted. Those thoughts are an attack from the darkest of all enemies. And Scripture takes this so seriously that it guarantees you will need armor to protect yourself against "the tactics of the Devil" (Eph. 6:11). Because this is a war, and often it takes place in our own minds—"our battle is not against flesh and blood, but against the rulers, against the authorities, against the world powers of this darkness, against the spiritual forces of evil in the heavens" (v. 12).

So step one for me is to sit up and get out of bed, out of that chair, out of the physical space where the sinful thoughts are overwhelming me.

Step two is to get myself into the spiritual room of my heavenly Father, just like my kids do when they're coming to find me to protect them from a bad dream. No matter how dark the night or how claustrophobic your thoughts, your bright and holy Father God is there with you—reach out and grab on to His hand. I do this by saying the name of Jesus, out loud to the dark. I call it out the way I would when I was calling my mom back in the days of my own childhood bedroom. I don't have to be loud. I can just whisper and I know He's there, opening a door in my mind to let the light in.

Because here's the thing I'm finally getting savvy to: just because I think it, doesn't make it true.

Every thought that comes through my mind does not have to be taken and trusted at face value. Just like my heart has had to make a comeback from years of spiritual poison, my mind needs the same treatment. I think we seriously and dangerously underestimate how much Satan hates relationship. How he despises friendship and all the ways it reflects the deep truth of God's holy Trinity.

From before time, Satan has conspired to twist and to taint what God has intended for good into something grotesque. Where we were intended to worship and hallow God, we worship ourselves and hallow our own image; where we were intended to love our neighbors as ourselves, we resent them and are jealous of them; and where our minds are made to love God with every cell and every thought—to "love the Lord your God with all your heart, with all your soul, with all your strength, and with all your mind" (Luke 10:27)—we instead spend hours spinning evil story lines about what others think, say, and intend for us and about us.

We are never in more dangerous territory than when we've been wounded by someone, and as we lie there bleeding and hurt, Satan tries to poke and prod and torture us into a reaction that is wildly out of proportion to the original wounding.

Because that is exactly his intention. It doesn't minimize the fact that we have been wronged and our hurt is true. But it amplifies that hurt in the middle of the night to provoke us into an unrighteous overreaction. I have had friendships that were hanging on by a thread, and if I'd let myself light the powder keg of frustration and bitterness that Satan had so sneakily planted in my mind during the night, there would have been no hope, no future, no blessing for either of us. The friendship would be been obliterated.

I find that often it's my most meaningful relationships, the ones I'm most desperate to put back together, that get the 4:00 a.m. treatment. But when I move both my body and my spirit out of the line of fire and into the truth of what Scripture says about me and about the way I'm supposed to love others, the battery slowly loses power. So as I sat wrapped up in a blanket, voicing my fears and then countering them out loud with the truth of Jesus, I could feel the tension and paranoia drain out of me.

> There is no fear in love (1 John 4:18).
>
> Love one another like Jesus has loved me (John 13:34).
>
> Forgive seventy times seven (Matt. 18:22).
>
> God keeps me safe in His house from accusing tongues (Ps. 31:20).
>
> I can cast all my anxiety on the Lord because He cares for me (1 Pet. 5:7).
>
> God is my hiding place and my shield; I will wait for His words before I rush into my own (Ps. 119:114).
>
> Be quick to listen, slow to speak, and slow to become angry (James 1:19).

Until slowly, sitting in the dark with the sun starting to gently warm the edges of the window frame, the last bit of tension seeped out of me and I could walk myself back to bed. My son was snoring in the same snuffled, familiar pattern as my husband, and they'd left me a sliver of the mattress to climb back into. The bed was warm and the air felt safe again, and I arrived dreamless into the light of day.

As I got the kids up for school and cycled my way through cereal for one, a sandwich for another, and an argument with the third one who doesn't like breakfast, I felt the sense of relief mounting. In the car on the way to the preschool drop-off, I knew deep down in the core of who I am that I had been saved by mere inches from being hit head-on by a semi-truck.

It's not the first time I've had this kind of experience. The kind where you're so wound up on your own sense of unfair treatment that you plot an entire conversation in your head or draft a long and detailed e-mail to the person who hurt you spelling out all the ways you need them to know that they were wrong or rude or inconsiderate or unkind. I've sat in front of that blinking cursor, heart racing and everything in me screaming, "They need to know that they are wrong and you are right." When something quietly blocked me from hitting send. I walked away and came back hours later to find everyday, regular conversation with that person still ongoing and plans unfolding, and if I'd hit send, I would have turned all that hope for relationship into so much shrapnel.

That pause, that extra moment of deliberate hesitation before giving in to my almost manic desire to stand up for myself, can be the heartbeat between a friendship's life and death. The moment right before the truck hits when someone reaches out a hand and drags you back to safety. It's a shock. It comes with scrapes and bruises, until I look up from the sidewalk and find I'm still alive and the friendship still has hope.

There is a time to share our hurts with people, for sure. There is a time to gently offer our broken bits and pieces and let them know we're wounded. But those tender conversations don't start out with accusation. If we want any chance of reconciliation, then our conversations have to start with compassion. A willingness to see the other point of view first, to love the other more than yourself. At 4:00 a.m., my fears and frustrations are not kind or gentle or others-centered. They're dictators that want to stomp a warpath right through the lives of the people who've hurt me. They're not helpful. They don't want future. They don't want friendship. They only want their own way.

And nowhere in Scripture are we given the promise of getting our own way. Instead, all through Scripture, the central theme from Adam to Noah to Abraham to Ruth to David to Jesus to the disciples to the nations to us is the theme of being redeemed by God for the singular purpose of becoming a witness of that same grace, mercy, and blessing to others. Over and over the promise is given that we are blessed so that we can become a blessing to everyone around us: "I will surely bless you and make your descendants as numerous as the stars in the sky and as the sand on the seashore. Your descendants will take possession of the cities of their enemies, and through your

offspring all nations on earth will be blessed, because you have obeyed me"
(Gen. 22:17–18 NIV).

God is wildly in love with even the people who might make us the craziest.
The people who are difficult and the people who are grumpy and unhelpful
and hard to understand. And sometimes those people are us. The most famous
of the apostles, Paul of the wild ministry and exhausting travel schedule and
the many churches he mentored, said, "Look at what is obvious. If anyone is
confident that he belongs to Christ, he should remind himself of this: Just as
he belongs to Christ, so do we" (2 Cor. 10:7).

That person you're so mad at, that person who has walked right over
some of your biggest feelings, well, if that person is a believer, then that
person belongs to Christ just as much as you. And so when I'm tired and
emotionally exhausted, I couldn't agree more profoundly with Beth Moore
when she says, "My feelings are at times such poor reflections of truth."[3]
Especially in the middle of the night. And the longer I spend time on this
planet surrounded by people who can rub each other raw like some kind of
human sandpaper, the more desperate I am to "let truth speak louder than
[my] feelings."[4]

Just because I think it, just because I feel it, doesn't make it true. And
sometimes the best way to figure out whether the story we're telling ourselves
in our head matches the reality that the other person is living is simply to ask
them. Brene Brown coined the powerful phrase "the story I'm making up,"[5]
and she uses it to defuse situations where one of the parties is about ready to
blow up because they feel so misunderstood and maligned. "It's a life-saver
for a few reasons, she says: 'It's honest, it's transparent, and it's vulnerable.'
Basically, you're telling the other person your reading of the situation—and
simultaneously admitting that you know it can't be 100% accurate."[6]

So when my friend Lisa and I had gone a few weeks of missed messages
and texts and long gaps, I was able to easily message her that the "story I'm
making up in my head is that you don't have time for me anymore now that
I've moved away." And she was able to laugh and reply that (a) I was crazy, and
(b) the reality is that she's become a full-time student with a full-time job as
well as a part-time job and full-time parenting and she barely has time to go

to the bathroom or sleep, let alone respond to my text messages the second I send them.

In the past, I've believed the stories I make up in my head 100 percent. But as I've earned more wrinkles and gray hairs, I've become a lot more skeptical about those stories. I'm learning that my own version is often the furthest removed from reality, and the more I let my feelings get worked up about my own interpretation of events without checking with an outside source, the more likely I am to break something—usually the feelings of the other person. So going to fact-check with that friend or with my husband or even with one of my kids, before I go off the deep end into my own cycle of frustration and blame saves us all a lot of drama. Giving the benefit of the doubt, believing their best intentions instead of my worst dramatic assumptions in the meantime, has saved a lot of unnecessarily hurt feelings.

But what about that person who's putting up walls? That person who isn't interested in your version of the story and who no longer feels safe. What do you do about that person and those conflicted feelings?

I take all those confused thoughts and feelings and dump them down at Jesus' feet. And then I ask Him to sort through them and show me which ones are true and which ones need to be brought into check because they're spinning wildly out of control. This is not wishful thinking. This is a promise that we can "demolish arguments . . . [by] taking every thought captive to obey Christ" (2 Cor. 10:4–5).

There will be some relationships that are so poisoned and bitter that we need to stop letting them feed us; we need to cut the ties and we need to walk away so that we can live. So that both of us can live. So that we can thrive in our individual lanes and keep running hard for the Kingdom. Those are often the relationships where it's impossible to have an honest, safe conversation about the different stories we're making up about each other. Those are the friendships where we need to recognize that we aren't ultimately responsible for the stories or the baggage the other person brought into the relationship. But we are responsible for moving ourselves out of harm's way and back into a place where we can flourish, away from the toxic poison that flowers in some relationships. And like we discussed together in chapter 6, sometimes that simply means letting go and going our separate ways. Trust Jesus to prompt you when that is what needs to happen. He will give you the wisdom to be able to tell the difference and the strength to make that choice.

But there are other friendships that are an assignment straight from Jesus Himself. That He's using to get up in your business and teach you some things about yourself. Some friendships where He's asking you to actually *be* His patience and grace and compassion personified in actual arms and time and conversations. Friendships where there isn't a shortcut to cutting out the tension that seems to have grown up out of nowhere between you. Being human comes with other human beings, so if we stop, drop, and cut them off any time we're offended, annoyed, frustrated, or unable to make sense of the current state of the friendship, we will soon enough find ourselves friendless and alone.

Yesterday, I sat down at my desk and made a list of the things I've lost because of friendships. Friendships have challenged me, pushed me out of my comfort zone, and forced me to look up from the solar system of my own creation where I've so regularly assumed I was the sun. The truth of it is that those friendships, the ones that have rubbed me raw as they've reminded me that I am not the center of the universe, have given me the gift of subtraction. We're so one-track minded when it comes to friendship—so programmed to look for what's in it for me—that sometimes we forget the best thing we can get out of a friendship might be one of the things we have lost because of it.

My hardest friendships have cost me. The love and patience they've required have cost me huge chunks of my pride. I've lost parts of my arrogance along the way and my inability to see the world from someone else's perspective. I've lost my unwillingness to compromise, and I've had to give up my stubborn refusal to apologize.

Some friendships are like a meat tenderizer. And sometimes that is what our hearts require. Our puffed-up, stubborn, arrogant hearts sometimes need the pounding, tenderizing mercy of a God who wants us to be malleable, capable of profound compassion, and quick to give someone else the benefit of the doubt.

I cringe when I think what I was like two decades ago—a completely self-involved, stubborn, and unintentional trampler of the feelings and sympathies of others. One particularly wretched memory I wish I could go back in time and change was the day I managed to make my secretary cry. I was a first-year associate at a law firm. I was also so clueless about my own role and life and purpose at the time that I was handicapped when it came to caring about the lives of anyone else. And on the day my secretary, twice my senior, started crying because of all the ways I'd treated her so thoughtlessly, no one was more surprised than me.

I was blind-sided, completely stunned that my behavior had had that kind of impact on another human being. And as this woman who could have been a friend to me voiced her feelings—this woman who spoke with such dignity about how I'd hurt her, how I'd disregarded her needs, and thoughtlessly walked all over her responsibilities—my ignorance grew bigger and uglier before my very eyes. If I could, I would go back and erase that moment. Instead, God has graciously given me the same opportunity over and over and over again in the faces of so many different friends to show kindness, compassion, and care in ways I failed to do back then.

I like to think—man, *I need to believe*—that those rough edges of my twenty-something self are slowly being sanded away by friends who've lived alongside me and rubbed off on me with their own generous grace where none was deserved. So that when those bumpy days arrive and you start to doubt your friends and it becomes hard to keep believing the best about them, I remember that sometimes the best work God does inside our souls is the most uncomfortable.

So on those days, on the days I am struggling to feel love, grace, compassion, or patience toward other humans, I ask God if I can borrow His feelings. If I can swap all my frustration for a slice of His worldview and a chunk of His feelings toward my fellow womankind. "This is God who can make us feel what we don't."[7] This is God who has loved them deeper and longer and who knows their rough edges and hurt insides better than we ever will. And this is the God who generously pours out His love and who never runs out and who is defined by compassion and speaks in grace—He walked the walk all the way to the cross and down into the dark tomb and out into the light again. With access to that kind of love, my own tired heart can be resurrected and keep opening up to keep loving while buried deeply and safely inside the shield of His own.

"For it is God who is working in you, enabling you both to desire [feel/want] and to work [act] out His good purpose" (Phil. 2:13). He will supply you with the feelings and He will do the work—in you and through you and for you so that you can be a blessing to the women around you instead of letting Satan explode a relationship that Jesus is trying to put back together.

The Power of Giving the Gift of the Benefit of the Doubt

I never cease to be amazed how Christ is in the business of restoring broken relationships and redeeming misunderstandings. Being willing to believe the best about the people in our lives while we're waiting on the broken to get fixed helps a hard process keep making progress. Because I'm a verbal processor, what I want to do is often the opposite of what is good for me or for that friendship that's currently going through the meat grinder. A lot of the time, all I really want to do is vent. I want to exorcise the feelings that are all churned up with ick and frustration so that I can feel better. And sometimes the feeling better is a slow time coming. So in the meantime I can easily go running to other women in our shared circle to vent it all out. To just let it all hang out and underline each and every way I've been wronged. While it might make me feel better in the moment, it's like eating that whole tray of brownies—the next morning you're gonna regret that choice. And you're gonna wake up feeling grosser than you did the night before.

So, instead, these days I'm trying to just sit still and feel my feelings. This is so much more impossible than it sounds. To just sit there and let the feelings of hurt and jealousy and anger and betrayal have their say. I listen to them. But I don't let them become the boss of me. I don't let them wipe out all the good work invested in a long friendship. I don't let them have the last word. And I don't believe everything they say. I listen. I pay attention. Because, "after years of being taught that the way to deal with painful emotions is to get rid of them, it can take a lot of reschooling to learn to sit with them instead."[8]

Then I slowly, slowly work my wounded mind around to giving my friend the benefit of the doubt.

This can be even harder than being willing to feel your hurt feelings. But it's the only way I know to keep my feelings from holding me hostage. From forcing me at angry, emotion-driven gunpoint to lash out and lash back. I deliberately make my mind give the benefit of the doubt to that friend because I know that it's the only hope I have of being understood myself. The hope that she'll take the time and exercise the will to give me the same benefit of the doubt when we're standing on opposite sides of a painful conversation.

Make no mistake—giving the benefit of the doubt to someone is a gift that will cost you. It's a hard cost to bear some days. But its reward can be priceless. And as I pause to process what I'm feeling, I've found that inviting one or two trusted friends into the journey with me is like having a friend below anchoring you while you're climbing a precarious rock face. It's not the same as gossiping or venting—which usually assume the other person is at fault and that you're the victim.

Giving the benefit of the doubt to someone is a gift that will cost you. It's a hard cost to bear some days. But its reward can be priceless.

Instead, inviting this kind of wise counsel into the conversation admits that you might have blind spots. It admits that you need an outside perspective to help you stay the course of believing the best about your friend while mining your own life for areas that need to change. I love how Proverbs puts it: "In abundance of counselors there is victory" (11:14 NASB). We need these kinds of friends because "their input and love for the person can mitigate against our pride, hurt, and irrational behavior as well as our own inexperience."[9] Because it's impossible to appreciate all the nuances by yourself. Impossible to know where she is, to appreciate the unique pressures in her life, to understand the backstory that might be the reason all that stress is seeping into the friendship.

Waiting and believing the best can be excruciating. Wise counselors with strong anchors are necessary. Because waiting while giving the benefit of the doubt can also save you from becoming your own worst wrecking ball.

Sometimes the waiting takes much longer than we would like. Sometimes there's no sign that your friend is returning the favor of believing the best about you. Sometimes, instead, it's clear that she isn't and that she's venting to people you care about. Some of the most painful months I lived through were one big season of waiting and wondering how on earth a friendship I'd been so sure of could have derailed so badly into distrust and misunderstanding. I wanted to defend myself, assert myself, and demand I be treated better. But instead, I listened to the wise friend who knew us both and who believed the best about both of us, and I let her feelings become my feelings for that season, so that I could believe the best even when I didn't feel like it.

And in the meantime, I quit trying to defend myself and trusted my reputation to Christ instead. It was a relief. It was still hard and hurtful, there's no getting around that, but we are called to love, to forgive, and to keep our hearts open. Scripture is crazy serious about this. It spells out literally—with no room for misinterpretation—what love requires: love "bears all things, believes all things, hopes all things, endures all things" (1 Cor. 13:7). Bearing, believing, hoping, and enduring through the long, dark days of believing the best about a friend is like boot camp for the soul.

For me, stubbornly giving her the benefit of the doubt and trusting the women who still trusted her was the hardest work I'd done on a friendship. Harder still because it's all done in private, with no one to bear witness to the sweat, guts, and determination it requires to take God at His Word over and over again. Only the Holy Spirit sees. Only the Holy Spirit knows how lonely it is. Only the Holy Spirit really gets it. But He is there. He will show up. He will keep offering fresh encouragement through wise mentors, and He will not let you down.

In my experience these seasons have surprise endings. Just when you think you can't take it anymore. Just when you're riddled with the inner tension of believing the best and enduring the loneliness of a lost friendship, He will surprise you—this God who has designed His planet and His people to be both the recipient as well as the conduit of His blessing.

I've heard versions of this same story told over plates of pizza and across a farmhouse table over shared chips and salsa. One friend said she thought it had been good-bye. She thought there wouldn't be room for restoration, but she never stopped praying. And four years later the shut door of a dear friendship creaked its way back open again. Another wise woman told the story of fifteen years spent interceding for a brutally difficult relationship at work. Transfer or resignation would have been her preference, but God kept her praying and at times begging Him for health, for life, for hope in this broken relationship. "Those are the kinds of prayers," she told me, "that God loves to answer."

Fifteen years later and the evening she told us the story, she'd just come home from a funeral. The funeral of her colleague's son. A funeral she still couldn't believe she'd been invited to attend. With the woman she's since held in her arms as they wept together. The woman who spent years refusing to talk to her.

For me, I was sitting in a small bakery over a bowl of soup when the e-mail popped up after months of silence. I could hardly click to open it, my hand was shaking so badly. My stomach seized up, and I felt a rage of emotions clogging up my throat as I read the subject line. I cried my way through every sentence. Because it had all been worth it. All the praying and the waiting and the believing the best. Let me tell you what I learned over a bowl of soup and my laptop computer and six stubborn months of choosing to believe the best. We cannot possibly presume to know what other people are living through. Life is so layered and complicated and beautiful and hard that even our best assumptions about someone else when laid against the truth of what they were living will never have been able to tell the whole story. And a lot of the time it's not even our business.

Our business is to believe the best about people. We are not their judge, their jury, and we are certainly not their god. We are intended to be their blessing. On purpose.

DON'T BE AFRAID TO LISTEN (EVEN IF YOU DON'T LIKE WHAT YOU HEAR)

"My inability to resolve conflicts well left a wake of broken and lost friendships. It was terribly isolating and lonely." —Anne[1]

I WAS LISTENING TO A podcast recently by two sisters who are also two of my favorite human beings—Emily P. Freeman, author of *Simply Tuesday*, and Myquillyn Smith, author of *The Nesting Place*. They were each taking turns answering listener questions but soon discovered that while one was sharing their answer, the other was inevitably not listening because they were too busy trying to think up their own answer. There was a lot of laughter and teasing about this unintended consequence.

Some days I think friendship feels like that.

Some days a friend is trying to share, and instead of laying down all the things we're mentally fiddling around with and instead of focusing our heads, hearts, eyes, and mouths on our friend, we're actually preoccupied with a sort of mental gymnastics planning what *we* want to say next.

Sometimes I imagine those conversations like this:

Friend: Gah, I'm so sad today. I feel stupid and dumb at my job, and there's this weird nagging loneliness I can't seem to shake.

Me: (internally thinking: Oh man, I know EXACTLY how that feels—this week has been the WORST. Just wait till I tell her about how I blew that deadline and how I'm sure my boss thinks I'm stupid and why won't my kids go to bed on time anymore.)

Friend: (takes a breath: —)

Me: Oh man, I know EXACTLY how that feels—this week has been the WORST. Just wait till I tell you about how I blew that deadline and how I'm sure my boss thinks I'm stupid and I don't understand why my kids won't go to bed on time anymore.

Friend: (stranded and without a way to steer the conversation back to the encouragement she so desperately needs just feels even lonelier instead)

Yeah, that. Which I think warrants a frank discussion about learning when sometimes it's *not* our turn to talk. And how listening is often the most powerful gift we can give a friend. Especially when they're trying to share something that feels vulnerable to them or that feels vulnerable to us—for example, when we've hurt them and they're trying to tell us about it.

Because sometimes our determination to speak before we're properly done listening is an act of self-defense. We load our responses, our arguments, and our words up in front of us to block out what's being said and lobby our own point of view out into the conversation instead.

Nothing will shut down true communication faster.

But nothing will disarm a friend more than the grace you grant them when you listen with palms up and walls down—inviting their hurt into your own self so you can understand it from the inside out.

Nothing is more powerful than giving someone the gift of truly hearing them without tagging on your own defensiveness, explanations, objections, or justifications.

Let's learn how to be proactive, non-defensive listeners.

7 Ways to Respond to Hard Conversations

I've been the community manager at the website www.incourage.me for nearly a decade. That means years of working with and for and alongside women. Writing about women, reading about women, talking to women, being in small (and large) groups of women.

I don't think I could possibly overstate how much I love women.

What a gift it is to serve them and how deeply I esteem their unique and varied callings as different from each other as you could possibly imagine and often just as deeply rooted in the same things—faith, family, and friendship.

In all my years serving that community, I've had the incredible privilege of hearing all kinds of interesting conversations as well as receiving lots of generous feedback. Feedback that's been encouraging, challenging, and sometimes difficult. Feedback in every possible form—e-mails, direct messages on Twitter or Facebook, Instagram tags, surveys at the end of conferences, phone calls, Google Hangouts, and text messages.

And in the past decade, I've learned more about processing feedback from others than in any other job I've held. I'd be remiss if I didn't share that learning. I think some of the best and hardest work God calls us to do is to love other people. In order to love other people well and genuinely, we must remember that the nature of being human means that we are going to bump into other beautiful human beings throughout the day so we need to be prepared for when we disagree. Or when what they share is hard to hear.

Some of the best and hardest work God calls us to do is to love other people.

We need to learn to be listeners with hands open rather than palms clenched in tight, frustrated, misunderstood fists.

If we want any hope of succeeding at what the disciple James called "the hard work of getting along" (James 3:17–18 MSG), then we need to work hard at listening well. And work even harder at responding with compassion and kindness. The kind that recognizes the people we live with, eat with, work with, or pass on the street are each made in the image of Christ and, therefore, should be treated with the same respect, care, and consideration as we would give Him.

Please don't assume I've got this all figured out. I'm bumbling and stumbling my way forward a lot of the time. But I figure if I can lend my bruises and scars and what they've taught me, then maybe you can avoid a few of your own. Because I know that Christ makes us family.

So here are seven things I have learned (and am still learning) when it comes to responding with love in the thick of hard conversations:

1. Check Your Place and Headspace

So often we think that we have to listen to a message or respond to an e-mail the instant we get it. And that fast response rate can accelerate an already heated situation. Friends, beware the smartphone that makes you trigger-happy.

Seconds. I have often felt the urgent need to respond to an e-mail, tweet, or other online request in seconds. No matter what I'm doing. I've been known to pull into a parking lot or ignore my kids at a family outing to quickly type out a response to an e-mail ping.

But after nearly a decade working in the online environment, I've realized that's just plain nuts. I don't work with nuclear launch code responsibilities. I'm not a heart surgeon. No one dies if I don't respond in five seconds flat. And, let's face it, any response typed out on a teeny screen in a Walmart parking lot is gonna be less coherent, comprehensive, and compelling than it probably deserves.

When someone wants to initiate a conversation that you know is going to be hard, I recommend making sure you're in the right place and headspace to be able to engage in a way that respects the conversation.

For example, I've learned never to open difficult e-mails or messages after hours when I'm already in my jammies and hanging out with the family. I know then I'm more likely to feel defensive, attacked, and vulnerable. But if I wait to read the message the next business day, when I'm dressed like I'm connecting with the writer in person, and in a headspace undistracted by bedtime stories and last glasses of water for the night, I'm much more able to read with an open heart and mind.

And if you're in person, there's nothing wrong with listening and, if needed, asking for time to process. You can schedule a time to follow up, admitting that you're not ready to respond right now, in the heat of the moment. And in the meantime, repeating back what you've heard as an act of affirmation to ensure that you've clearly understood what was communicated is response enough. Hard conversations deserve time and thought, and sometimes neither are forthcoming in the moment. Don't be afraid to take the necessary time to process.

2. Be Quick to Listen and Slow to Speak

I'm always staggered by how fast my reflex is to defend myself or justify my position. To talk back fast before anyone can get another word in. To force myself to be understood. And to get angry when I am not.

But that is not the advice the Bible gives. Instead, James again wisely advises: "My dear brothers and sisters, take note of this: Everyone should be quick to listen, slow to speak and slow to become angry" (James 1:19 NIV).

This is not easy. Period. It is not easy to open your ears and close your mouth. It is not easy to sit at the table and let a friend talk and talk and talk and really try to hear her and understand her fears. It is not easy to go back and reread an e-mail to make sure you really did understand what was being said—and not what you assumed was being said. It is not easy to give someone the benefit of the doubt. It is not easy to willingly put my own agenda on the back burner and make myself listen.

But listening is one of the most powerful tools we have when it comes to defusing a hard conversation. Making someone feel heard helps take the sting out of their frustration and opens the door for dialogue. Defending yourself lights the fire. Listening to someone else helps put it out.

Defending yourself lights the fire. Listening to someone else helps put it out.

3. Pause. Literally.

Dish up another round of mashed potatoes. Take a slow bite of food. Hold on to your coffee cup and swallow without rushing to speak first. Close Twitter. Shut down Facebook. Pause the voice message. Tell the person on the other side of the conversation you need a moment to really absorb what they've said.

Tell your friend, your boss, your family member, your women's ministry leader, your book club friend, or whomever it is that you'd really appreciate the time to process. Then, when you do respond, you will be sure to have done their point justice. Breathe in. Breathe out. Take a walk. Hug your kids. Look out the window. Remind yourself that even this doesn't constitute an emergency to God.

4. Pray

Take any hurt feelings or frustrations to God first. I'm certain He can take it. Tell Him all the bad, shouty feelings you are having and let Him filter them through His hands and His words and His grace to you. He has, as the good prayer says, forgiven us our debts first so that we might forgive our debtors.

Take Him literally on this. He won't let you down.

And if the conversation is happening in real time instead of by e-mail or social media, still pause to pray. One of the most powerful responses I've experienced to an angry, hard, conversation caught me completely off guard with prayer. I was the frustrated one and the fellow female leader I was talking to—after she had listened to all my anger and frustration, after she had thanked me for sharing it with her— simply asked if we could please quickly pray before she responded.

It disarmed me completely. I will never forget it, and I will aim to honor her example by learning from it.

5. Ask for Advice

Test your response on someone else first. Your husband, a good friend, a mentor, your pastor. Don't trust yourself when you're responding to something hard. Invite someone you trust to tell you if you've overreacted or if your response is appropriate. To give you feedback on the wording and tone of your answer.

I've been known to draft an e-mail and make myself wait at least overnight before I send it. There's something about coming back to the conversation in the morning that can change your perspective, make your heart more tender, and give God time to show you what you missed or misunderstood the first time around.

6. Respond

Let's not leave each other hanging when hard conversations are unfolding. Let's respond in a timely, loving manner. Let's assume the best about each other. Let's give each other the benefit of the doubt. Let's start from a position of love: believing all things, hoping all things.

Let's be lavish in our willingness to see the other point of view.

Let's be wildly, generous grace givers. Let's be unprecedented in our willingness to encourage, to try again, to walk around in someone else's shoes.

There's nothing so powerful as an apology when one is necessary, a gentle word to turn away anger, and an openness to truly listen to someone else's stories.

Because the stories that other people offer us—no matter how hard they might sometimes be to receive—are always a gift.

We only have to remember to see them as such.

7. Don't Be Afraid to Say Sorry

While we can't control other peoples' stories, we are responsible for our own roles in them. So when you discover that there's a friend who's been hurt or offended or left out because of you, and you are convicted by the Holy Spirit that you were in the wrong, then regardless of the inconvenient timing, just drop everything. Everything. Right then and there pick up your phone or open an email or write a card to make it right. Go and do that first. Go and inconvenience yourself to make a friendship right.

The Bible is pretty radical about this. In Matthew 5:23–24, Jesus says, "So if you are offering your gift on the altar, and there you remember that your brother has something against you, leave your gift there in front of the altar. First go and be reconciled with your brother, and then come and offer your gift."

And then the commentary notes, "Speaking to the context of His day, Jesus said disciples should seek reconciliation even if it meant halting in the middle of offering sacrifices (an example of what would have constituted very urgent business) at the Jerusalem temple. This interruption was significant since Jesus' original audience (located away from Jerusalem) would have to abandon their gift at the altar, travel for days to reach Galilee and seek reconciliation, and then return to Judea to complete the sacrifice. Such is the priority of reconciliation."[2]

We don't like being inconvenienced. We especially don't like being inconvenienced by circumstances that are awkward, tense, uncomfortable, and liable to explode in our faces. No wonder so many of us go through life with a big ball of unresolved conflict bumping around in our wake. And we think if we just keep moving forward long enough or fast enough or with big enough blinders on we'll outrun it. But it's tied to us. This big, sticky gob of bad feelings and suppressed hurt, and unresolved bitterness. I think we get so used to hauling that thing around that after a while we adopt it. We take in this pet of broken, past relationships and we feed it all our current scraps of bitterness and frustration, and one day we're surprised when it turns around and roars with such vehemence we feel it's hot, sticky spit fly into our faces and watch in surprised horror as it savages us with massive jaws.

No wonder the Bible tells us to "throw all spoiled virtue and cancerous evil in the garbage" (James 1:21 MSG). To cut ourselves free of that burden of broken relationship that's been bumping along at our heels and instead to "let our gardener, God, landscape you with the Word, making a salvation-garden of your life" (v. 21 MSG). A salvation-garden! A place full of life and freedom, full of forgiveness and safety, a place beyond the thorns of false guilt and bitterness, far away from the sinking sand of comparison and insecurity. A garden of shade and welcome, a garden lush with acceptance and security, with warmth and a hundred daily do-overs, fresh starts and the chance to keep being the friend who would never unfriend someone else for her own convenience. Because, "whoever catches a glimpse of the revealed counsel of God—the free life!—even out of the corner of [her] eye, and sticks with it, is no distracted scatterbrain but a . . . woman of action. That person will find delight and affirmation in the action" (v. 25 MSG).

This isn't a foolproof method. This isn't a guarantee that you'll make it through that conversation or family reunion without bumps and bruises on your heart. This is simply a beginning. An intentional beginning that can help you be prepared. Help you process before you speak. Help you remember that not all hard conversations are bad conversations. And that you don't have to get sucked into the same cycles that repeat every year around your table.

PART 4

WHERE DO WE START?

Do the Hard Work of Getting Along

There's no sugarcoating it. Friendship can be terribly hard work. So I really appreciate the Bible being super frank about that. In fact, Jesus' own brother wrote these words explaining just how hard it can be to live out healthy friendships—I feel like he really gets it:

> Real wisdom, God's wisdom, begins with a holy life and is characterized by getting along with others. It is gentle and reasonable, overflowing with mercy and blessings, not hot one day and cold the next, not two-faced. You can develop a healthy, robust community that lives right with God and enjoy its results *only if you do the hard work of getting along with each other*, treating each other with dignity and honor. (James 3:17–18 MSG, emphasis mine)

And often it's that very hardness that makes us think we're doing it wrong. But the thing is, that hardness is a compass pointing us in the direction of what we're doing right. Because it means we haven't quit yet. It means we've decided to stick. It means we're choosing not to unfriend with the swipe of a finger, but instead to give the gift of the do-over. It's so worth it. Because it becomes the gift we didn't realize we're actually giving ourselves.

Here's the thing about women. They may be wearing purple boots or skinny jeans or sweat pants. But when they do that thing—that thing where they look right into your eyes, where they just reach over and hug you, where they whisper secret truths in tears that trail slowly down their cheeks, where they surprise you with a packet of Twizzlers, where they lend you their lipstick, where they aren't afraid to babysit your screaming baby, where they compliment your hair.

Yeah, that thing they do? It's magical. It's the kind of superpower that can turn a day inside out. What women can do for one another. How they can heal each other with the power of laughter. And hospitality that's contagious. Sometimes we're so busy wondering if we're getting it right, so busy worrying we're not measuring up, so caught up in thinking we need to be just like her that we forget she loves us just the way we are.

She loves the joy and Jesus and friendship and tired-up-all-night-with-the-baby eyes that make you, you. Forget awkward, forget feeling small or insecure or worried about what she's thinking.

Jump.

Just jump.

Women have the power to catch you in their I-know-just-what-you're-talking-about smiles, their encouragement that it gets easier or better or that God-will-hold-you-when-it-doesn't empathy.

Let them. Open your heart, your hand, your home. Forget making them look perfect. Just invite a friend in. Take a risk. It might be the best kind of worth it.

This invitation is for the hurt women. The wish-they-had-sisters women. The why-wasn't-I-invited women.

This is for the girlfriends and heart friends and long-distance friends and miss-my-friends friends.

This is for the women who love long afternoons catching up and slow Saturdays on the sofa splitting the last brownie, the first story, the hard memory.

This is for the sisterhood, the motherhood, the neighborhood, the misunderstood.

This is for the places that got broken by the friends who wouldn't forgive, couldn't move on, didn't hear our hearts.

This is for the old wounds, the fresh hurts, the questions and prayers and midnight pleas; for the women hoping for a do-over, a safe place, a friend who gets all the unique wonder wrapped up in you.

This version of friendship is a true story, an old story, the same story that we've all been living. This is the hard choice of staying committed to our friends, our communities, our dreams, and our God who is the crossroads where all these broken places are connected, mended, restored, and intimately comprehended.

This kind of friendship is the gift. It is the going first. It is the testimony of the brave who chose friendship in spite of fear. This is the loud voice of comparison squashed down, drowned out, overcome by a choice to love, to love, to love because Christ first loved us.

This brave choice is the laying down of jealousy, the raising up of encouragement. This is the cheering for someone else and feeling the powerful joy in return.

This is where it's okay to cry. This is where we cup your cheeks and your heart and your stories. This is where we nod our heads and open our arms and say, "Me too. Yes, me too."

This is the hard work of getting along.

This is friendship on purpose.

PRACTICE BEING A FRIEND TO YOURSELF TODAY

"I have believed that I'm not the real deal. That somehow I am fooling myself into believing that I have been saved. I know that Jesus said I am His. That if I believe and confess, that I am His. No one can pluck me from His hand. Not even myself."
– Lindsey[1]

THERE ARE SO MANY things I'm not good at. And apparently I have an inner monologue determined to record each and every one of them. There's a voice in my head that tells me I am not enough. Some days it's quiet and some days it's super shouty. It's the strangest thing to discover the back of your brain muttering mean things to yourself.

The whisper is so soft, so ordinary, so normal by now that I rarely stop to investigate. I just let the words run through my veins until they seem like a normal part of my DNA. This house will never be clean. You'll never get caught up on the laundry. Your words won't match up to hers. You've never lived up to your New Year's resolutions. You're never going to get caught up. You're going to start another week already behind the curve. You're just not good at this.

Maybe you can relate? And if that weren't bad enough, we trick ourselves into believing we're the only ones who fail at All. The. Things. And then we beat ourselves up. And tell ourselves mean things at the end of long days. Days spent meeting deadlines and helping rake the neighbor's yard. Days spent studying and commuting and writing and catching up with long-distance friends and grandparents around the corner. Days spent keeping tiny humans alive and thriving.

When we've cooked and cleaned and commuted and brought home the bacon and washed and cleaned some more and checked the homework and sung the songs and read the books, we sit down on the sofa and shake our heads and tell ourselves what bad, bad moms or friends or daughters or roommates or wives we are.

That's insane. And exhausting.

And in case you thought you were the only one, here's a small taste of the crazy that runs in a wild and vicious loop through my mind at the end of any given day:

- You should have added pureed spinach to dinner tonight.
- You should have remembered to buy spinach.
- You should have been meal planning for the last four years so that spinach could have made it onto the shopping list.
- You shouldn't have let the kids watch TV while eating last night. Or this morning.
- You should be having more meaningful dinner conversations.
- You should read more.
- You should watch TV less.
- You should enjoy your family more.
- You should lose your patience less.
- You should volunteer at church.
- You should wash the sheets more regularly.
- You should eat less ice cream.
- You should exercise more.
- You should go to bed earlier.
- You should be like her.

You should.

You should.

You should.

Until my head is about to split right open. Until I forget that I showed up. I parented. I made dinner. I worked hard. I had meaningful conversations, and I belly-laughed till I snorted today. But I forget all that when I hear that voice list all my "should-haves" and "not-good-enoughs."

I heard that voice in the car today. I was sitting in a parking lot in our minivan. Alone. Maybe that's why I listened without just letting it wash over me. Maybe that's why I tuned in to the nefarious whispering I'd been letting slide until then.

I listened and I almost couldn't believe what I heard. I was surprised, actually. Kind of amazed that I was capable of such petty meanness to myself. Because the thing about that voice is that it is a nitpicker. It delights in destroying the DNA of a day, a dream, a moment bit-by-petulant-bit.

But when I tuned in, it sounded more and more like static. Fuzzy, harsh, unforgiving, and small. My friend Holley Gerth calls it devil static—the noise that tries to drown out the truth God is speaking into our lives and through our lives. The noise that crackles and cackles and tries to poke fun at who we are becoming—tries to derail us out of sheer embarrassment.

I told that voice off today.

Yes, I talked back to myself in an empty car. To those lies I was saying to myself, I spoke out loud the words that have been spoken over me by The Word. By the voice who speaks the only words that matter: "For we are God's handiwork, created in Christ Jesus to do good works, which God prepared in advance for us to do" (Eph. 2:10 NIV).

I called out that voice with all its mean and miserable words. And in doing so I could almost hear it deflate. I addressed that no-voice with my whole attention, listing my inheritance in Christ (Eph. 1:11), my royal claim (1 Pet. 2:9) because of Jesus, my significance because I am His. Because He is enough, I am Chosen, Cherished, and Beloved. And I could hear the static fizzling.

I am not nothing.

You are not nothing.

We are daughters of the King. We are bought at a price. We are loved. And there is a much greater voice, a voice with all the rich, resonant tones of Truth so filled with love for us that unlike that static, He will rejoice over us with singing (Zeph. 3:17 NIV). With *singing*. Not hissing or criticizing or comparing or mocking, but with singing.

We must believe that voice of Truth with all the faith we can muster if we want to be the kind of friends who can be trusted not to unfriend others. It starts with us. The words we say to ourselves matter because the God who is The Word says we matter. And it's time we start believing Him.

It's time we start asking Jesus to help us see ourselves through His eyes and His Word. To teach us to show kindness toward ourselves and compassion toward others. Because until then—until we can look ourselves in the mirror and see ourselves through the lens of love—we won't have the practice necessary to love others. To love the hurting people around us who have believed all manner of lies about themselves. Lies that have grown out of broken friendships and hurtful relationships. Lies that can sprout out of something as seemingly innocuous as 140 characters in a tweet or Facebook status update that still cuts like a knife.

But sometimes the worst lies we believe about ourselves have originated in our own heads. We believe we've failed to live up to the love and trust Jesus has given us and we're desperately hard on ourselves while at the same time shrugging our shoulders in defeat, because we simply don't trust ourselves to do better.

> *The words we say to ourselves matter because the God who is The Word says we matter. And it's time we start believing Him.*

"Separated by two thousand years and nothing at all, Peter and I, and many others, go out and weep bitterly together because we fail our Master and because he always knew that we would."[2] And like Peter, I am awkward and dripping with my own insecurity when Jesus calls me again past all my insecurities and into the new identity He's given me—His own. So that I can stop worrying about myself and be brave enough to believe that He might want someone like me, someone like you, to go and feed His church. Because after all, the "Bible tells the stories not of a series of beaming, airbrushed heroes, but flawed, confused, geniuses/idiots who got it right and then got it wrong."[3] And Jesus stuck by them. He'll stick by me too. And by you. He will never unfriend us.

Do you believe it? Can you be convinced that nothing could make the God who gave up His title, His throne, His realm, and His only Son for you *ever* consider unfriending you? That nothing can separate us from that kind of radical love (Rom. 8:35–39)? Not being unfriended by your closest friend or accumulating a million likes, not the wildest success or the most public, social shaming. Neither today nor tomorrow, nor any headlines, neither pushing all the limits of this life nor sinking to its most depraved depths, nor anything else on the web, in your church bulletin, or at the local PTA meeting, or what was whispered at the book club this week.

Neither Facebook nor Twitter, mean girls nor church cliques will be able to separate us from the radical, never-giving-up, never-looking-back, always-believing-the-best love of God. A love that was made tangible, that took deep breaths in the flesh-and-blood body of Jesus Christ who literally moved into the neighborhood just to have that chance to be up-close-and-personal friends with you and who has promised that He will never leave you nor forsake you.

Neither Facebook nor Twitter, mean girls nor church cliques will be able to separate us from the radical, never-giving-up, never-looking-back, always-believing-the-best love of God.

Believe it, friends. Believe it before you can be a friend. Be willing to believe it for the sake of your friends and the desperate sake of your own lonely heart. And on the days your doubts are louder than your belief, then trust the Holy Spirit to believe it on your behalf. Take this truth and deposit it, use super glue if necessary, into the very core of who you are so that you will never have to fear being abandoned, rejected, or left out. Until we have that truth cemented into the foundation of our identity, we will not be able to give friendship our all. Real friendship, friendship that doesn't hold back, friendship that always believes the best. For that kind of friendship, you need to believe it first for yourself. Go first. Believe that you're beloved. Be your own best friend today.

Because you can wear the boots and worry over the not-so-skinny jeans and whether or not your eyeliner looks trendy-messy or just plain messy when what you're really looking to apply is a big, bold, red stamp of approval.

But here's the thing: you already are. You actually already are friended. No matter how you look or what you say or whether or not you figured out the right necklace to wear with that black top, you've been perfectly picked by the God who makes no mistakes.

You with the tired eyes and up-all-night baby.

You with the job that you messed up on this morning or the project assignment that's got you tied up in knots.

You with the tender bank balance and the kids who won't mind and the mind that feels like it's about to explode.

You with the worry or the regret or the love squandered or lists forgotten.

You with the aging parents or lost mother or forgotten father.

You with the family infighting or too-long commute or too late to school to be there in time to meet him for lunch like you'd promised.

You with the gray hairs and extra pounds and shy story and lonely eyes.

You, you, you.

Beloved. Chosen. *Friended* every single one.

Not because of your size or status or number of Facebook friends. Chosen not because of your name or your business card or parenting prowess. Wanted not because of your social currency or number of credit cards or square footage of your house.

But because God is forever love (Jer. 31:3). Always, infinitely interested in you, His daughter, right down to her dirty bathtub rings and worry about tomorrow. He's been coming for you since the beginning of time, and He's not about to give up now.

PRACTICE BEING A FRIEND TO SOMEONE ELSE TODAY

"The only way to guarantee never making friends is never trying again." —Kristen[1]

THE THING ABOUT FRIENDSHIP is that it takes work. A lot of work. It takes practice. It takes showing up. But when we keep showing up in the small things, those eventually become the big, life-changing things that can happen in one neighborhood between two streets.

Our friends will anchor us and preach Jesus to us simply by showing up, by helping out, by meeting kids at the bus stop, and by bringing over a meal. By washing our dirty dishes and inviting us into their mess; friends teach us that we belong to a God who moved into the neighborhood and can be seen clearest through the tangible hands and feet and faces and play dates and late nights with the real-life people He's placed in our everydays.

> *Our friends will anchor us and preach Jesus to us simply by showing up.*

These are the friendships that will preach to our daughters.

This is the legacy we get to leave them every day in between the school lunches and sports practices. One that models what it looks like to love other women well. Generously. With open hands and open doors and messy houses and lives and honest words and second, third, fourth chances.

I am learning what it means to be a good friend because I am becoming a student of friendship. I study the women around me and watch what it looks like to BE the friend. They teach me what good neighboring looks like for us here in the middle of the everyday ordinary. Even, and especially, on the days I don't have it together when I'm hurting and insecure, or when I'm without excuses or hope. On those days, I have a friend who comes and finds me and wraps me up in her neighborliness, and it's the kind of friendship you can actually feel. She is my living, breathing, Bible definition of friendship. If I wanted to teach you what it looks like to be a friend to someone else, I wouldn't give you a to-do list; I'd introduce you to the women who are teaching me about friendship.

These are the friendships that will preach to our daughters.

I hadn't slept in about three nights when Lisa knocked on the door. I hadn't washed my hair in as many days. Or showered, for that matter. I was wearing the pink T-shirt that I never wear in public. Soft and comfortable, but not presentable—especially if you don't have a bra on underneath. One sock on, one off, my sweat pants tangled around me. The nightstand covered in cough drops, tissues, and an assortment of medicines; I'd coughed my way into walking pneumonia and had an aching side that made it hard to breathe, to laugh, and impossible to answer the door.

But my boys heard the knocking. It was just a dull, dim, annoying ache from the next room. I'd been ignoring my cell phone for an hour because all that mattered was that my children had let me keep sleeping after nights of not sleeping and the heat of the cough had banked down to a slow burn. But the ringing phone had now morphed into a persistent knocking on the door and my kids wouldn't ignore that.

No contact lenses in, hair in a rat's nest, I saw her outlined in the bedroom door frame, and what's a girl to do other than sit up?

Turns out I'd slept through an hour of what should have been the kids' play date. And I was supposed to have dropped them off, but instead I hadn't woken up, hadn't fed them or dressed them, and I still couldn't see properly, or breathe, or think.

I grabbed the first real shirt I could find and dragged it over my head and rasped my hellos and sorrys and promises to deliver them when I was actually dressed and coherent. But while I rambled, this "love-you-even-though-you-forgot-me" friend was telling me in the background that she'd drop them off, and I was nodding in her direction, because really she was still just a blur to me but the outlines of her friendship were solid. I could see them.

What I couldn't see was the long list of everything I was supposed to do that day because my daughter had broken the arm off one side of my glasses. So I had to squint into the rest of the day while holding hard my aching ribs and painfully swallowing when necessary. Control is an illusion we women grab hold of tightly. We white-knuckle wanting things to go the way we planned them. We like our lists because they make us feel safe and productive and make us think that if we can just write it down, then we know it will turn out just so.

I had my long, reliable list and then I overslept. My children hadn't been fed and it was 9:45 and they opened the door to unexpected neighbors and embarrassed me with their complete lack of embarrassment.

That's the old Sunday school story in real time, isn't it? With its trick question—"Who is my neighbor?" And you probably know it too, the answer that comes back in the tale of the good Samaritan and the challenge to actually *be* a good neighbor, and to quit worrying about who qualifies as your neighbor.

Just go be a good neighbor, already, Jesus says (Luke 10:25–37).

That woman, the one who stood on my doorstep, organized my children, jumped into my chaos, took over my plans, gathered up their sweatshirts, and told me she'd feed them, understood.

I hugged her and tried not to cough on her. I did it all with my eyes half blind. Lack of contact lenses and gratitude both making it hard to see properly through the grace of friendship.

I closed the door. I headed back to the bedroom. Still coughing. She called later to tell me my boys got drenched in mud at the playground. Because, of course. But that she put all their clothes in the washer, since she figured I didn't need more laundry on my hands. And asked if the boys could stay for lunch while the clothes dried.

I turned on the shower and just stood under the hot water letting the steam wipe away the sweat from the struggle. I let go of my lists and my expectations and attempts to control the people around me and just stood in quiet, reverent thanks. For friends who show up.

THE NEVER UNFRIENDED
PROMISE

I promise I will never unfriend you.

Not with the swipe of my finger, not with the roll of my eyes, not with a mean word said behind your back, or a circle too small to pull up one more chair.

I choose to like you.

I choose to choose you. To include you. To invite you.

Even on the days we hit road bumps. I don't want another friendship breakup. I want a friendship that won't give up.

So, I give you my too-loud laughter and my awkward tears.

I give you my sofa for the days you just can't even. And the nights you need a safe place to feel heard without saying a word.

Let there be coffee and long conversations.

Let there be messy, ordinary Tuesdays where neither of us is embarrassed by our dust bunnies.

I won't try to force our friendship into jeans that won't fit.

I won't treat you like a quick fix.

I will like you just the way you are.

Because I believe in guilt-free friendship.

And on the days we're tangled up in our own insecurities, let's agree to give each other the gift of the benefit of the doubt. Wrapped up with the giant bow of believing the best about each other, even when we don't feel like it.

I'm sure I won't always get it right.

But I'll keep showing up.

With encouragement instead of competition. With Kleenex, big news or sad news, on the bad hair days and the Mondays, and all the in-between days with their ordinary news too.

Friendship on purpose.

Here's to me and you.

WITH THANKS

I T WOULD BE IMPOSSIBLE to list the names of all the women who have shaped my friendship journey. Writing this book has reminded me how friend-rich I am. I am so 100 percent in all your debt. Thank you for taking me, loving me, and changing me. And a particular thank you:

To my childhood friends in South Africa: Adene, Bernadette, Dorothy, Gertrude, Liza, Melanie, Rozanna, Vanessa, and Xenia.

To the women from Gordon College: Aida, Heather, Ingrid, Kristen, Leslie, Nicole, Sara, Tara, and Tiffany.

To the women from Notre Dame Law School—the GQs: Amiee, Becky, Janelle, Jill, Katherine, Marjie, Maureen, Melissa, and Shonda.

To the women from Ukraine: Colleen, Heike, Ira, Lesya, Mariah, Masha, Oksana, Roxanne, Valya, Wendy Lu, and Zee.

To the women from 3CI and Take Action: Annelien, Cathy, Crystal, Jonna, and Joy.

To the strong and beautiful women from my family: Wanda, Annie, Carine, Chloé, Lulu, Megan, Mo, Petunia, Tshepiso, and baby Mackenzie Jo. Debbie, Kim, Jill, and Emily.

To the Tuesday night girls: Christy, Connie, Janice, Karine, and Lisa.

To the women from Bethel: Alice, Alinda, Leyla, Grace, Kim, Mandy, Ruthie, and Simone.

To my boss lady friends: Chelsea, Sarah Mae, and Meg.

To my agent, Lisa. Thank you for always being my friend above all other things.

To the LifeWay/B&H team: Angela, Becky, Faith, Jennifer, Heather, Michelle, and Paige.

To the incomparable DaySpring team: Anna, Becky, Denise, Katie, Kim, Mary, and of course Saul.

To the women who've never been afraid to speak truth into my life with a side of tender encouragement: Ann, Bobbi, Christie, Elise, Holley, Jessica, Kristen, Lisa, and Stacey. I'm so grateful you are the voices in my head.

To the writers and community of (in)courage. Thank you for trusting me with your stories. Thank you for teaching me about friendship. Thank you for making me a better writer and more importantly, a better friend.

To Peter, the best friend of all. Thank you for giving us three such amazing tiny humans whose friendship we get to foster and enjoy. Jackson, Micah, and Zoe—may your friendship outlast these wonderful days when you still all wanted to crash in the same room. Take it from your mom, there's no friend like those who are related to you.

Zoe, a special word to you, my precious daughter. Friendship is always worth it, so when it comes to mean girls, try giving them the benefit of the doubt—meanness is usually a symptom of something else, not a condition in and of itself. And yes, I pinky promise to always be your best friend.

And to Jesus, who started this whole thing—becoming my friend before I even knew Him. Thank You, in all the years since, for never unfriending me.

NOTES

Part 1

1. See http://www.incourage.me/2012/06/youre-right-christian-women-and-incourage
-writers-arent-immune-from-cliques.html#comment-1823719192.

2. Henry Cloud and John Townsend, *Safe People* (Grand Rapids, MI: Zondervan, 1995),
Kindle location 1233.

Chapter 1

1. See http://www.incourage.me/2012/04/fact-christian-women-will-hurt-you.html.

2. Henry Cloud and John Townsend, *Safe People* (Grand Rapids, MI: Zondervan, 1996),
Kindle location 2448.

3. Ibid.

4. See http://www.incourage.me/2015/02/the-worst-breakup.html.

5. Daniel Goleman, *Social Intelligence: The New Science of Human Relationships* (New York:
Bantam Dell, 2006), 69.

6. Leslie Parrott, *Soul Friends: What Every Woman Needs to Grow in Her Faith* (Grand
Rapids, MI: Zondervan, 2014), 13.

7. Goleman, *Social Intelligence*, 11.

8. See http://www.incourage.me/2012/04/why-you-need-to-find-community-even-when
-youre-really-hurting.html#comment-1823712356.

9. See http://www.incourage.me/2012/06/youre-right-christian-women-and-incourage
-writers-arent-immune-from-cliques.html#comment-1823719092.

10. See http://www.incourage.me/2015/03/when-youve-been-hurt-by-women.html#comment
-1898931467.

11. Goleman, *Social Intelligence*, 10.

12. Dr. Nathan Ogan, *Paul's Letter to the Romans* (Los Banos, CA: Providentia Books,
2015), 20: "Legalism is described in Scripture as being like having a dead person strapped to
your body going with you wherever you go." He goes further to explain in the footnote to that
sentence, "Cf Romans 7:24 where Paul brings to mind spiritual death as being similar to carrying a dead body. In ancient Rome, the Emperors were well known for their creativity in thinking
up dreaded forms of punishment such as binding the corpse of a murder victim to the back of an
accused murderer." Also, *Barnes' Notes on the Bible* states, "Some have supposed that he refers to
a custom practiced by ancient tyrants, of binding a dead body to a captive as a punishment, and
compelling him to drag the cumbersome and offensive burden with him wherever he went. I do
not see any evidence that the apostle had this in view. But such a fact may be used as a striking
and perhaps not improper illustration of the meaning of the apostle here. No strength of words
could express deeper feeling; none more feelingly indicate the necessity of the grace of God to

accomplish that to which the unaided human powers are incompetent." See http://biblehub
.com/commentaries/barnes/romans/7.htm.

13. See http://www.kerysso.org/public/page127.htm.

14. Goleman, *Social Intelligence*, 308.

15. Ibid.

16. See Beth Moore, *Get Out of That Pit: Straight Talk about God's Deliverance* (Nashville, TN: Thomas Nelson, 2009), 42.

17. Ibid.

18. Ibid.

19. Ibid., 47.

20. Ibid.

21. Ibid., 45.

22. Ibid., 47.

23. Goleman, *Social Intelligence*, 308.

Chapter 2

1. See http://www.incourage.me/2012/06/youre-right-christian-women-and-incourage
-writers-arent-immune-from-cliques.html#comment-1823719120.

2. Marina Keegan, *The Opposite of Loneliness* (New York: Scribner, 2013), 1.

3. Barna Group, "How the Last Decade Changed American Life," July 31, 2013.

4. See more at: http://lisajobaker.com/2015/04/7-ways-for-women-to-find-soul-friends
/#sthash.WYsifHar.dpuf.

5. Barna Group, "How the Last Decade Changed American Life," July 31, 2013.

6. See http://www.ncbi.nlm.nih.gov/pmc/articles/PMC1121917.

7. Ibid.

8. Ibid.

9. Tim Keller, "Adoration: Hallowed Be Thy Name" Podcast, http://www.gospelinlife.com
/adoration-hallowed-be-thy-name-6377.

10. The Westminster Catechism.

11. See http://www.incourage.me/2015/03/six-ways-to-banish-fomo.html#comment
-1885122161.

Chapter 3

1. See http://www.incourage.me/2012/06/youre-right-christian-women-and-incourage
-writers-arent-immune-from-cliques.html#comment-1823719045.

2. See http://www.incourage.me/2012/11/when-you-wonder-why-everyone-else-seems-to
-have-friends.html#comment-1823690932.

Part 2

1. Jan Karon, *Come Rain or Come Shine* (New York: G. P. Putnam's Sons, 2015), 92.

2. See discussion of *shalom* in the context of loving others in Part III: What *Can* We Do about It.

3. Beth Moore, *Get Out of That Pit: Straight Talk about God's Deliverance* (Nashville, TN: Thomas Nelson, 2009), 118.

Chapter 4

1. See http://www.incourage.me/2016/02/listening-to-those-who-are-different-from-us.html#comment-2508140542.
2. Henry Cloud and John Townsend, *Safe People* (Grand Rapids, MI: Zondervan, 1995), Kindle location 2991.
3. Ibid., Kindle location 3037.
4. See https://twitter.com/bobgoff/status/699618542140796928.
5. *Safe People*, Kindle location 2996.
6. See http://www.incourage.me/2016/02/listening-to-those-who-are-different-from-us.html.
7. Shauna Niequist, *Bread and Wine: A Love Letter to Life Around the Table with Recipes* (Grand Rapids, MI: Zondervan, 2013), 132.
8. Pulpit Commentary, http://biblehub.com/commentaries/john/17-12.htm.
9. Margery Williams, *The Velveteen Rabbit* (New York: Delacorte Press, 1922).

Chapter 5

1. See http://www.incourage.me/2012/06/youre-right-christian-women-and-incourage-writers-arent-immune-from-cliques.html#comment-1823719145.
2. Timothy Keller, *The Freedom of Self-Forgetfulness* (UK: 10Publishing, 2013), Kindle location 323.
3. Henry Cloud and John Townsend, *Safe People* (Grand Rapids, MI: Zondervan, 1995), Kindle location 2955.

Chapter 6

1. See http://www.incourage.me/2016/09/when-you-have-to-say-the-hard-thing.html#comment-52083.
2. *Safe People*, Kindle location 1428 (emphasis mine).
3. Ibid., Kindle location 2935.
4. Ibid.
5. Ibid., Kindle location 2938.
6. Ibid., Kindle location 2940.
7. Ibid., Kindle location 2942.
8. Ibid., Kindle location 2946.
9. Ibid., Kindle location 2949.
10. Ibid., Kindle location 2957.
11. Ibid., Kindle location 1075.

Part 3

1. See http://biblehub.com/hebrew/7965.htm.
2. Kevin DeYoung and Greg Gilbert, *What Is the Mission of the Church? Making Sense of Social Justice, Shalom and the Great Commission* (Wheaton, IL: Crossway, 2011).
3. Ibid., 31.
4. Rick Ezell, "Sermon: Being a Peacemaker," www.lifeway.com/Article/sermon-blessed-peacemakers-sons-god-matthew-5.
5. 1 SHEMU'EL—1 Samuel 17:18: "And carry these ten cheeses to the captain of their thousand, and look how your brethren are in shalom, and take their pledge," http://www.yahwehsword.org/scriptures/09_samuel_shemuel/117_shemuel_samuel.htm.
6. Ezell, "Sermon: Being a Peacemaker," http://www.lifeway.com/Article/sermon-blessed-peacemakers-sons-god-matthew-5.

7. Henry Cloud and John Townsend, *Safe People* (Grand Rapids, MI: Zondervan. 1995), Kindle location 2170.

Chapter 7

1. See http://lisajobaker.com/2013/03/being-brave-enough-to-be-un-fine/#comment-107830.
2. See http://lisajobaker.com/2013/03/being-brave-enough-to-be-un-fine/#comment-107809.
3. Rachel Simmons, http://time.com/3637044/teen-girls-bff-best-friends/.
4. Henry Cloud and John Townsend, *Safe People* (Grand Rapids, MI: Zondervan, 1995), Kindle location 1230.

Chapter 8

1. See http://lisajobaker.com/2015/04/7-ways-for-women-to-find-soul-friends/#comment-253583.
2. Myquillyn Smith, *The Nesting Place* (Grand Rapids, MI: Zondervan, 2014), 59.
3. Leslie Parrott, *Soul Friends* (Grand Rapids, MI: Zondervan, 2015), 203.
4. Shauna Niequist, *Bread and Wine: A Love Letter to Life Around the Table with Recipes* (Grand Rapids, MI: Zondervan, 2013), 195.
5. See http://zizzivivizz.com/2013/02/12/between/.

Chapter 9

1. See http://www.incourage.me/2015/06/the-friends-who-come-to-carry-you.html#comment-2087414773.
2. John Blase, *Know When to Hold 'Em: The High Stakes Game of Fatherhood* (Nashville, TN: Abingdon Press, 2013), Kindle location 561.
3. Anna Whiston-Donaldson, *Rare Bird: A Memoir of Loss and Love* (New York: Convergent Books, 2014), 89.
4. Ibid., 103.
5. Ibid., 105.
6. Ibid., 106.
7. C. S. Lewis, *A Grief Observed* (1961; repr., New York: HarperOne, 2015), 57.
8. Adrian Plass and Jeff Lucas, *Seriously Funny* (Milton Keynes, UK: Authentic Media, 2010), Kindle location 868.
9. Ibid., 866.
10. Christie Purifoy on Instagram, https://www.instagram.com/p/BBa4uuav_bV/?taken-by=christiepurifoy.
11. See http://www.shaunaniequist.com/enough-part-2/.
12. Oswald Chambers, *My Utmost for His Highest* (1935; repr., Grand Rapids, MI: Discovery House, 1992), March 3, "His Commission to Us."
13. Plass and Lucas, *Seriously Funny*, Kindle location 336.

Chapter 10

1. See http://lisajobaker.com/2013/04/comparisons-will-kick-you-in-the-teeth-and-hijack-your-dreams-every-time/#comment-108993.
2. Priscilla Shirer, *Fervent: A Woman's Battle Plan for Serious, Specific, and Strategic Prayer* (Nashville: B&H Publishing, 2015), 55.
3. Ibid., 57.
4. Henry Cloud and John Townsend, *Safe People* (Grand Rapids, MI: Zondervan, 1995), Kindle location 935.

5. Ibid., 941.

6. Ibid., 931.

7. Shirer, *Fervent*, 57.

8. "Christian Rapper Lecrae Asks: 'Do You Understand Your Value?' in Speech to Millennials about 'Reflecting the Glory of God'", http://www.christianpost.com/news/christian-rapper -lecrae-asks-do-you-understand-your-value-in-speech-to-millennials-about-reflecting-the-glory -of-god-139172/

9. Plass, *Seriously Funny*, Kindle location 456, 458.

Chapter 11

1. See http://www.incourage.me/2012/06/youre-right-christian-women-and-incourage -writers-arent-immune-from-cliques.html#comment-1823719068.

2. C. S. Lewis, "The Inner Ring," Memorial Lecture at King's College, University of London, 1944.

3. Ibid.

Chapter 12

1. See http://www.incourage.me/2012/06/youre-right-christian-women-and-incourage-wri ters-arent-immune-from-cliques.html#comment-1823719161.

2. See C. S. Lewis, *The Screwtape Letters*, 9.

3. Beth Moore, *Get Out of That Pit: Straight Talk about God* (Nashville, TN: Thomas Nelson, 2009), 53.

4. Ibid., 259.

5. See http://www.techinsider.io/brene-browns-biggest-life-hack-is-a-simple-phrase-2015-8.

6. Ibid.

7. Beth Moore, *Audacious* (Nashville, TN: B&H Publishing, 2015), 74.

8. Barbara Brown Taylor, *Learning to Walk in the Dark* (New York: HarperCollins, 2015), Kindle location, 164.

9. Henry Cloud and John Townsend, *Safe People* (Grand Rapids, MI: Zondervan, 1995), Kindle location 193.

Chapter 13

1. See http://www.incourage.me/2016/02/terrible-at-friendship.html.

2. E. Ray Clendenen and Jeremy Royal Howard, eds., *Holman Illustrated Bible Commentary* (Nashville, TN: B&H Publishing, 2015), 1014.

Chapter 14

1. See http://www.incourage.me/2016/03/what-if-you-were-kind-instead-of-critical-to- yourself-today.html#comment-45659.

2. Adrian Plass and Jeff Lucas, *Seriously Funny* (Milton Keynes, UK: Authentic Media, 2010), Kindle location 568.

3. Ibid., Kindle location 504.

Chapter 15

1. See http://www.incourage.me/2012/02/when-you-need-friends-but-have-a-hard-time -finding-them.html.

Helping women find a place of

faith, connection & friendship

At (in)courage you are always welcome,
just the way you are.
You're surrounded by grace,
loved unconditionally and never alone.

Whether you're single or have great-grandkids.
Whether you're a mama, an artist, an
entrepreneur, or a book lover. Whether you
stay at home or work full time. Whether you're
outgoing or prefer an afternoon alone.
Come share. Come connect.

You'll always find yourself among friends.

(in)courage

Gifts, Stationery & Cards

Listening to the Lord
and our community
helps us create products
that equip you to make
meaningful connections
with other women.

Available in retail stores
&
dayspring.com

The Bible Study to find yourself among friends!

WE SAVED YOU A SEAT

Finding and Keeping Lasting Friendships

(in)courage community manager

LISA-JO BAKER

AVAILABLE MAY 1

Friendship is hard. It takes vulnerability, service, and active participation. In a world where women often feel as if they need to wait for the perfect time and place to connect, God wants us to pursue friendships just as we are with the people He's placed in our lives.

In this 7-session Bible study, Lisa-Jo Baker explores our relationship with Jesus as a model for friendship—the kind that shapes us into the image of Christ. Nothing transforms us like the impact of a friend because it's how Jesus radically and intimately connects with us. So instead of hiding behind "fine" we need to overcome the fear of being known just as we are and find the courage to connect.

WeSavedYouASeat.com

Lisa-Jo Baker

is convinced that the shortest distance between strangers
IS A SHARED AWKWARD STORY.

Connect with her at **lisajobaker.com** and receive access to her **FREE library of prints and videos.**

She'd love to connect with you and swap stories!

WEB HOME
for free resources & speaking requests
www.lisajobaker.com

INSTAGRAM
@lisajobaker

TWITTER
@lisajobaker

FACEBOOK
www.facebook.com/lisajobaker

Lisa-Jo lives just outside Washington, DC, with her husband and their three very loud kids, where she connects, encourages and champions women in person and online through her honest take on life and her ability to laugh at herself and learn out loud from her mistakes.

She is the author of *Surprised by Motherhood* as well as the Bible Study, *We Saved You a Seat*, the creator of *The Temper Toolkit* and her writings have been syndicated from New Zealand to New York including on Huffington Post Parents, BlogHer, Desert News, Focus on the Family, Stroller Traffic, iVillage, OH Baby!, the Power of Moms, and Christianity.com.

As the community manager at the website incourage.me since 2010, Lisa-Jo has had the chance to engage hundreds of conversations with women about friendship. And it never gets old.